SHETLAND BUSES
IN THE 20TH CENTURY

by
Gordon M Jamieson

NOSTALGIA ROAD

NOSTALGIA ROAD PREMIER SERIES

CONTENTS

Cover Pictures (repeated this page):

Front: R.G. Jamieson's Mulliner-bodied OB, PS 1999, driven by James John Jamieson along the road from Cullivoe towards Gutcher in snowy weather.

Rear 1. Hunter of Baltasound's Bedford OB, SY 8878

Rear 2. Johnson Bros. Burlingham Seagull, HMS 227 at the garage in Brae.

Rear 3. Pat Isbister's Bedford SB5-Plaxton Panorama, FWT 321C.

Rear 4. Eunson's AEC Reliance 633 WKL, with Harrington Cavalier body.

Rear 5. John Leask & Son's 'Town Service' with 951 EVT an ex-PMT Bedford.

Rear 6. Shalder Coaches Volvo, LPS 850V at the Scalloway garage.

The **Nostalgia Road** Series™
is conceived, designed and published by
Trans-Pennine Publishing Ltd.
PO Box 10
Appleby-in-Westmorland
Cumbria, CA16 6FA
Tel. 017683 51053
Fax. 017683 53558
ISDN. 017683 53684
e-mail trans.pennine@virgin.net
(A Quality Guild registered company)

Reprographics
Barnabus Design & Repro
Threemilestone, Truro
Cornwall, TR4 9AN
01872 241185

And Printed in Cumbria by
Kent Valley Colour Printers Ltd.
Shap Road Industrial Estate
Kendal, Cumbria LA9 6NZ
01539 741344

SHETLAND BUSES - A FOREWORD.

It was a great honour and privilege to be asked by Gordon Jamieson to write a brief foreword to this exciting, and copiously illustrated new book, *Shetland Buses in the 20th Century*.

I have known Gordon for many years and both of us have been involved with buses all our lives. However, to Gordon, buses are not merely tools for doing a job, they are a big part of his life, and each one is treated almost as an individual. Therefore he has spent many hours researching the buses that have been worked by the Shetland operators, and collecting photographs of them. Gordon's collection of photographs is, I am sure, unique in the bus world. The amount of work and research he has put in over the last 25 years building up the collection is immense. I have spent many a happy and sometimes long night with Gordon trying to sort out the Leask fleet. Mind you, a dram or two would always be on hand to help move things along!

Gordon went to great lengths to obtain photographs and results were forthcoming from many parts of Shetland and beyond. Over the years hundreds of people have helped, few with the thought of any reward, save the satisfaction of seeing the illustrations appearing in a book one day. Often the pictures that he found were not primarily of a bus, and the vehicle would be seen occupying a small space within some larger image. Summer outings and Sunday School picnics yielded several images of happy groups with the illusive bus being quite incidental in the background.

Gordon's ambition has, for many years, been to publish his collection in book form and I am delighted that he has finally achieved that with the help of Alan Earnshaw and others. For my part I was very happy to be asked to use our offices and travel agency on the Esplanade in Lerwick for the actual launch of the book.

My grandfather, John Leask was the first person to operate a bus in Shetland with 13 seats. That was back in 1928, and I wonder what he would think now if he could see what has followed on from that. Like Gordon's grandfather, who was a pioneer in bringing public transport to the Island of Yell, John Leask started a business that has seen many changes, and carried thousands of passengers over the years. Our respective grandfathers could not have envisaged the way that things would have developed by the end of the 20th-Century, but I am sure that they would be very proud of the bus fleets that still bear their names today.

The intervening years have seen good times and bad, happy passengers and sad, and above all a series of progressive changes. Sometimes change came quickly, and at others it dragged its feet, but all these changes are recorded in this publication. I wish Gordon every success with this splendid book. It is, as I said, a unique book and one that should have a very wide appeal both in Shetland and in the greater world beyond.

Peter R. Leask
John Leask & Son, Lerwick
November 2000

UNST

BLUEMUL SOUND

FETLAR

YELL SOUND

YELL

OUT SKERRIES

ST MAGNUS BAY

PAPA STOUR

WHALSAY

MAINLAND

FOULA

LERWICK

BRESSAY

The

Shetland

Islands

INTRODUCTION

I suppose this book had its beginnings many years ago, probably far longer than I care to remember really, as I started collecting the photographs used herein when I was just fifteen years old. It all began when I decided to collect pictures of all the vehicles we had owned in our family business of coach and taxi hirers at Cullivoe on the island of Yell. If you look at the map opposite, you will note that Yell is the second most northerly inhabited island in Britain, for only Unst lays beyond us, and beyond that comes the bleak waters of the North Atlantic.

To those readers who live in the Shetland Islands, the area will need little description, but for those from the south I must explain about the geography of the islands before continuing with my story. In all, the Shetland Islands comprise around one hundred islands, of which just 16 are inhabited. The map opposite shows the location of the islands that make up Shetland, but to the majority of people in Britain this unique group is just a small dot that appears on the top of the TV weather map. The largest of the islands is simply known as The Mainland, in which the capital and administrative centre is Lerwick. Originally the main centre was Scalloway, and this remains as the second largest town in the islands. The other main centres of population are Brae and Sandwick. The main harbour is located in Lerwick, whilst the main airport is in Sumburgh at the south end of The Mainland.

In recent years the coming of North Sea Oil has brought considerable change to Shetland, not least of which was the construction of the massive oil terminal at Sullom Voe. This is one of the largest oil terminals in Europe, and has its own dedicated facilities for the ocean-going bulk tankers that come to collect the crude oil pumped ashore by the pipelines connecting with the North Sea platforms. The story of the oil boom will be well known to many, so suffice it to say that the creation of Sullom Voe drastically affected the islands and brought many improvements in local infrastructure, including shipping, air services, road improvement and, in the case of my industry, a significant change in the way bus services were operated.

Above: *The Jamieson 'fleet' at Cullivoe in 1955, showing from left to right: GM 3384 a Vauxhall 14 used on taxi work, PS 2421 an 11-seat Morris Commercial mini-bus, CGE 200 a 1939 Bedford ML with a Duple 14-seat body, LKJ 885 an Austin K2SL with a 17-seat Kenex body, and YJ 8939 a Bedford OB with a 27-seat Plaxton body.*

The construction of Sullom Voe began in the early 1970s, and was completed within the decade. As a result of this, and other improvements, the islands enjoyed an expansion of its public transport network, notably the coming of the inter-island car ferries that replaced the older passenger-only ferries (as seen in some of the photographs that follow). This then brought more convenient transport links to the remote islands like Papa Stour, Fair Isle and Out Skerries. Even so, quite a number of islands remain without internal bus services, whilst others have only recently seen public transport in the form of the Royal Mail Post Bus service.

Prior to the coming of the car ferries, coach operators ran what was known as The Overland Service, with service buses and coaches linking up the various ferry services. The Overland Service is still in being today, but the coming of the ro-ro ferry service considerably opened up the frequency of travel, and the ability for folk from many of the islands to commute to work into Lerwick or Sullom Voe. This did have an effect on bus services, as car ownership grew, but despite all the pressures and changes, an adequate public service is still provided on Unst, Yell, Fetlar, Whalsay, Burra Isle, and Bressay.

This of course was a time of change, and as I saw these things take place, I felt that someone should be recording them. So, as I collected the pictures of our own vehicles, I also began to beg, borrow (and almost steal) any picture I could find that showed any of the buses and coaches that had worked on Yell. I made a natural cut-off point of anything under 13-seat capacity, as it became difficult to draw a line where a taxi/hire car ended and a mini-bus began. And, having started on Yell, I decided to expand my horizons to include Shetland as a whole!

As the 1970s progressed, so did my collection of vehicle photographs, and already it had become a valuable record as I was helped considerably by other operators and enthusiasts who had recognised that bus services in Shetland were unique! In many ways what existed here, at least in public transport terms, was something of a time warp. Indeed the islands were the final working place of buses and coaches that had become extinct in mainland Britain, as older models were sacrificed on the altar of modernity. Hence, buses and coaches that still had many years of life left in them came north to eke out their days. The Bedford OBs and SBs, Austins and Fordson chassis were ideal for island operation, with their smaller capacity and economical running.

Such vehicles joined those that had come new (or relatively new) to the Shetland Islands at the end of World War II, and they lasted well into the late-1970s. That is not to say that new vehicles did not arrive, and this was especially so in the early to mid-1970s, when the grant regime was favourable to the purchase of new service vehicles; our own Bedford YRQ-Duple Dominant (HPS 28P) is an example. Yet, in the islands we liked to make our vehicles last and almost 25 years on, this coach is still in daily service on Yell and running almost as good as it did when new!

As newer vehicles came, and the roads improved, so the need to retain the older examples became less important, and one by one the old models were cascaded down from the larger operators to the smaller ones, and then finally taken out of service and sold for summer houses, greenhouses, wood sheds and peat stores. Many of these remain today, albeit in a terribly derelict condition. Yet, their existence has had two remarkable effects, one of which ultimately led to the publication of this book!

In the autumn of 1999 I had a visit from Philip Lamb, the editor of *Preserved Bus* magazine, who came north to photograph these relics for his magazine. After a visit lasting several days, he returned south promising to 'get things moving' in respect to these buses and coaches that were so desperately in need of saving. The article duly appeared in his magazine, and it showed two coaches that I had also stored away for future preservation, a Bedford SB (KWX 412) and a Bedford VAS (BJX 848C). Within a few weeks Philip had introduced me to Alan Earnshaw of Trans-Pennine Publishing, and things really began to move!

In March Alan, and his brother-in-law (Mike Berry of the Mersey & Calder Bus Preservation Group) came to visit me in Cullivoe, and plans were made to get my two coaches back to West Yorkshire where they had first originated. The plan was initially a straight-forward sale, but as the days progressed I began to realise that here was a way in which I could still maintain my involvement in the two coaches that I had longed to preserve, but had never had the time to do so. By the end of March, the Viking Coach Trust had been formed, and in June 2000 BJX 848C was entered in the **Shetland Classic Car Show**. At the end of July it went south for restoration, and I look forward to the day when it returns to Shetland in its full glory. As this was the first coach that I ever bought for our company, I make no excuse for spending some time talking about it, and also dedicating the whole of page 19 to showing photographs of it.

The departure of BJX 848C marked the start of this book, as Alan then took the opportunity to examine my photograph collection. Recognising it as a unique record, he agreed to publish my work as a pictorial history of Shetland Buses in the 20th Century; for by the time he had come to examine the collection, I had managed to collect a picture of almost every bus and coach to work on the islands in service or hire work. The only major exception were those passenger vehicles brought in to transport construction workers at Sullom Voe, and military transports operated in World War II. I also excluded those firms bringing tour coaches to Shetland, so that this remained a pure record of island operators.

Now, as you will imagine, the photographs of some vehicles proved hard to find, even some from recent years, so at times I have had to sacrifice quality for the sake of providing a visual record. At other times I have had to use the same picture twice, in order to show a photographic record of it with another operator. The choice of pictures has not been easy, but I hope you will agree with my choice as I have endeavoured to show every vehicle that has been in each operator's fleet. As a consequence there is little room for much text to explain the record, but I hope you will agree with me, that it does indeed display a complete and highly fascinating Pictorial History of *Shetland Buses in the 20th Century*.

Below: *The Jamieson fleet at Cullivoe in 1983, with ex-Sinclair SB (KWX 412) second from the left, of this line-up the first three coaches have now been preserved.*

Gordon M. Jamieson, Cullivoe, November 2000

The island of Unst is the most northerly of all the inhabited islands in Britain, and so it forms a logical place to commence our story. The island has a wide variety of geological formations, and is thus a most attractive place to visit. During the late 19th and early 20th centuries, the population increased from around 500 to over 10,000 as the harbour at Baltasound became the base for around 600 herring boats. This went into decline in the 1920s and the island's population is around 1,000 today.

J. G. HUNTER & SON.

This firm ran a total of seven buses from its base at Baltasound between 1950 and 1974, when they were taken over by P. Y. Mills Coaches. The fleet, in a blue and cream livery, was as follows:-

Reg.	Chassis	Body	Cap.	Year	Acq.
PS 1595	Bedford WD	local made	B14F	1947	1950
AMS 240	Bedford OWB	SMT	B28F	1944	1951
CAV 269	Bedford OWB	SMT	B28F	1944	1953
FBU 149	Bedford OB	Plaxton	C30F	1949	1956
BKS 179	Bedford OB	Mulliner	B28F	1950	1960
SY 8878	Bedford OB	Duple	C29F	1948	1968
EMS 825	Bedford SB	Burlingham	C31F	1953	1970

Above: *In full colour, we see FBU 149 by the ferry terminal at Belmont, awaiting the boat to Yell in the latter part of the 1950s.*

Centre Right: *This is PS 1595 a Bedford WD chassis no.33430 with a local conversion to the body. This vehicle came to Shetland as an ex-WD lorry with a square tin front of the type fitted to many army Bedfords during the war. The body came from an ex-MacBrayne's Morris Commercial that had been purchased by R. A. Sandison of Brae. The two parts were joined into one new bus by P. J. Smith of Sandwick in 1947. Smith operated it until 1950, when the B14F went north to Unst.*

Bottom Right: *The end of PS 1595, following withdrawal in 1956, it lay derelict in front of Hunter's house for many years.*

Above: *The second bus in the Hunter fleet was AMS 240, a Bedford OWB (22845) with a Scottish Motor Traction (SMT) B28F body. This 'utility' bus was built in 1944 and arrived in Unst at the age of 7-years from John Leask & Sons in Lerwick. It was scrapped on the island in 1964.*

Right: *A further view of AMS 240 at Britain's most northerly post office (which became something of a tourist attraction), with driver Boofie Hunter on the left and Magnus Sinclair on the right!*

Left: *CAV 269 was the third vehicle in the fleet, and it was once again a Bedford OWB (18067) with a SMT utility body. This was almost identical to AMS 240, and representative of many rural buses all over Britain in the immediate post-war era. It came to Hunter from Johnson's of Scalloway in 1953, and it remained in service for a further seven years before being scrapped in 1960. The picture shows the coach in its days with Leask's of Lerwick, who operated the coach between 1945 and 1951, when it was sold to Johnson.*

Right: *The fourth member of the fleet was FBU 149, another Bedford, but this time sporting the forward-control OYB designation and carrying chassis number 91911. It had the full-front Plaxton body (563) and achieved extra seating capacity over the traditional OB layout. As a result FBU 149 had 30 seats as opposed to the normal 27, 28 or 29 found on other body types. It is seen here outside the Baltasound Hotel, which has the distinction of being the most northerly hotel in the realm. As for the coach, it came to Hunter in 1956 from Leask's and was scrapped in 1968 at the age of 19 years.*

Left and Opposite Page Bottom Right: *Moving on to Hunter's fifth vehicle, we see BKS 179 in good times and bad. This was another Bedford OB (117160), but this time with a Mk.II Mulliner body. This was a 27-seat service bus with the builders number of T500, and it had the distinction of being fitted with luggage racks. It first came to Shetland to join the fleet of W. Thomson of Sandwick in 1950, when it was just a year old. It passed to the trustees of T. R. Manson (Yell) in 1952, before going to Unst eight years later. It was finally scrapped in 1967. The picture on the left shows it at Hunter's garage, whilst that on the right shows it off the road between Haroldswick and Baltasound in snowy conditions, despite having snow chains fitted to the rear wheels. No-one was hurt!*

Above: *Another superb view taken by an unknown visitor in the late 1960s, possibly in the summer of 1969. Like many of the pictures collected, purchased and donated over the years, I have no record of who made this contribution, but I am sure you will agree with me that all these anonymous contributors deserve a deep debt of gratitude. Although we are unable to record the names of individual contributors, I trust that they will appreciate their work finally coming into print after so many years. This view shows SY 8878, the penultimate member of the Hunter fleet at Belmont pier as the ferry* Tystie *(Tystie is the Shetland name for a black guillemot) arrives from Gutcher. The Bedford OB (88725) with a Duple Vista C29F body (52217) was purchased in 1968, when it was already 20 years old. Hunter acquired this coach from James Watt & Son Reawick, who in turn had purchased it from Johnson of Scalloway. The coach had a very short life with Hunter, and it was scrapped in 1970 when a Bedford SB was acquired.*

Above: *Hunter's final purchase was a Bedford SB (15063), which was fitted with the attractive Burlingham Baby Seagull 31-seat body. This coach (EMS 825) was originally built in Blackpool in 1953, and I understand was new to Alexander of Falkirk. It was purchased from Alexander Northern in 1970 and bought at a time when Hunter was needing to modernise his fleet. With the assistance of John Leask & Sons it was brought from mainland Scotland to Lerwick, where it was re-painted in a blue and cream livery. It was then sent north to Unst, and this involved two sea crossings in the days before the ro-ro ferries. The need for a bus of this size and quality was quite obvious when the island tour work is considered, as tours of Yell and Unst were quite popular. Decent vehicles were required to connect with the ferry services, as passenger 'expectations' had become quite high in the early 1970s. Not only were such tours run by Leask's, but they also brought up distant operators like Scotia Tours, Wallace Arnold and Midland Red. The SB although a little long in the tooth lasted until 1974 when Hunter sold out to P. Y. Mills. The SB stood outside Hunter's garage for a further 24 years and was finally cut up by the Shetland Island Amenity Trust in 1998.*

J. W. LAURENSON

J.W. Laurenson (pictured inset) ran a total of four buses from his base at Norwick and, like Hunter, he was also in business between 1950 and 1974, before being taken over by P. Y. Mills Coaches. The fleet, in a blue and cream livery, was as follows:-

Reg.	Chassis	Body	Cap.	Year	Acq.
GS 4634	Bedford WLB	Duple	C20F	1934	1950
CRG 462	Bedford OB	SMT	C27F	1947	1958
KGB 759	Bedford SB	Brush	C33F	1952	1967
2810 AC	Austin LD02A	Kenex	B13F	1958	1972

Above: *This Bedford SB (1094), whilst looking like a Duple Vega, is actually fitted with a Brush C33F body. Registered KGB 759, it came to be the third vehicle operated by Laurenson after it was purchased from Leask's in 1969. It transferred to P.Y. Mills in 1974.*

Right: *The first vehicle in the Laurenson fleet was GS 4634, a Bedford WLB (109536), which is just seen behind the boat sail. It was fitted with a Duple C20F body and dated from 1934, when Bedford had only been making buses and coaches for three years. It came to Unst as late as 1950, having been bought from Yell where it had been operated for just one year by H. R. Williamson of Sellafirth. It is seen here at Uyeasound Regatta in the early-1950s. It was finally scrapped in 1958 after a very full life.*

Above: *The second Laurenson coach, was a Bedford OB (43267) with a SMT 27-seat body. He purchased CRG 682 from Swallow of Aberdeen in 1958, and it was finally scrapped in 1969.*

Right: *This view of the last member of the Laurenson fleet, features an Austin LD02A (25581) with a Kenex 13-seat body. New in 1958, 2801 AC came to G.W.N. Williamson of Gruting in 1964 and was passed on to Laurenson in 1972. It was scrapped in 1974 when the business was acquired by P.Y. Mills.*

P. Y. MILLS COACHES

As noted earlier, the two Unst operators, Hunter and Laurenson, both sold out to a new concern P.Y. Mills in 1974, but both fleets were pretty well run down by that time. Out of the vehicles still running at that time only KGB 759 was kept in service. Even then this vehicle lasted for just two years before being sold to an operator on the island of Whalsay - however the SB-Brush was never re-painted into the new red and cream colour scheme adopted by P. Y. Mills Coaches, Baltasound. This firm was eventually sold out to P & T Coaches in 1996, and their fleet list was as follows.

Reg.	Chassis	Body	Cap.	Year	Acq.
KGB 759	Bedford SB	Brush	C33F	1952	1974
WBO 992K	Bedford VAS5	Duple	C29F	1971	1976
OPS 550X	Bedford YMQ	Duple	C35F	1981	New
C239 VPS	Bedford YMP	Plaxton	C35F	1985	New
H253 ANE	Ford Transit	Deansgate	C15F	1990	New
A373 JSA	Dodge	Reeve Bur	C39F	1984	1995

Centre Right: *Pictured outside our new garage at Cullivoe, is WBO 992K a Bedford VAS5 (IT486323) fitted with a Duple Vista 25 C29F body (231-40). It was built in 1971 and bought in 1976 from Venn of Cardiff. It was purchased in a red and cream livery, and this was adopted by Mills for their future coaches. The picture was taken at our garage in 1978 when the coach was brought across for re-painting. It lasted in service for a further three years and was finally scrapped at Baltasound in 1981.*

Bottom Right: *The first new vehicle to be purchased by P. Y Mills was OPS 550X, a Bedford YMQ (LW451538) fitted with a Duple Dominant II C35F body (151-1575) with Express specifications (note the double doors). Once again a red and cream paint scheme was adopted. After four years service it was disposed of to the dealers Yeates of Loughborough, in exchange for another new coach C239 VPS. From Yeates the Bedford was sold on to Wake of Sparkforth, but is seen here during its time at Baltasound.*

Above: *A further view of KGB 759, this time after it was purchased by P.Y. Mills in 1974. The SB did not last long and was duly sold to T. A. Arthur of Whalsay in 1976.*

Left: *Mills' fourth vehicle was this Bedford YMP (FT106726) with a Plaxton Paramount 3200 C35F (858MQP-2C016), which was purchased from Yeates of Loughborough in 1985. As will be noted C239 VPS shows a slight change in the colour scheme with orange replacing the former red. The coach is seen when relatively new at the Belmont Ferry Terminal. This was doing the Unst parts of Overland Service (from Belmont to Haroldswick), and included the carriage of the Royal Mail after it had been brought across by the ferry. The mail service goes back many years, but at the time of writing it has just been handed back to the Post Office, who have started to run dedicated Royal Mail vans. It will be noted that this vehicle is a considerable improvement from the OB operated on the same Overland service at the end of the 1960s and is seen on page 9. When P.Y. Mills sold the business to P & T Coaches in 1996, C239 VPS was passed over to the new operator and is still in service at the time of writing.*

Right: *This coach, A373 JSA was actually the last acquisition by Peter Mills, who purchased it from the Royal Air Force at RAF Saxa Vord. It was a Reeve Burgess bodied Dodge (SDF G13A90), built to 'military specifications' and providing 39 seats. Due to the high entry steps it was not much used in service, and saw only a nominal amount of private hire work. It then went on to P & T Coaches when the business was sold and is still at their garage at Baltasound, but is no longer in use.*

Below: *This Ford Transit mini bus with 15 seats was an obvious answer to many of the service needs on Unst, and like elsewhere in the Shetland Islands, the use of such small buses has become common place. Whilst some enthusiasts may not like to see such vehicles included in bus books, one must remember that this is a record of all 13+seat service vehicles used in Shetland. This example, H253 ANE (chassis no. BDVVLL 78362) has a Deansgate body. It was new in 1990 and passed to P & T Coaches at the time of the takeover in 1996, and it is still in daily service with them.*

P & T COACHES

The final (and sole remaining) operator on Unst is P&T Coaches of Baltasound who acquired the business of P.Y. Mills in 1996, taking over the three vehicles noted before. The livery was changed to yellow, blue and white, after the firm purchased a Ford Transit in this livery from James Watt & Son, Reawick; in the years that followed the fleet list became:-

Reg.	Chassis	Body	Cap.	Year	Acq.
C239 VPS	Bedford YMP	Plaxton	C35F	1985	1996
H253 ANE	Ford Transit	Deansgate	C15F	1990	1996
A373 JSA	Dodge	Reeve Bur	C39F	1984	1996
H845 AUS	Ford Transit	Deansgate	C14F	1990	1996
D741 WRC	Ford R1014	Plaxton	C45F	1987	1996
R924 OPS	Volvo	Plaxton	C45F	1998	new

Above: *Another of the vehicles acquired from P. Y. Mills was C239 VPS a Bedford YMP (FT106726) fitted with a Plaxton Paramount 3200 C35F body (858MQP-2C016) which was built in 1985. It is seen here at the Gutcher Ferry Terminal after crossing the Bluemull Sound on the ro-ro ferry Geira, which is operated (like the other inter-island ferries) by the Shetland Islands Council. Ferries depart from this terminal for both Unst and Fetlar. Apart from a Royal Mail estate car, which carries passengers on mail routes, Fetlar is devoid of scheduled bus services.*

Above: *Seen in the livery of James Watt & Son, Reawick, this 14-seat Transit (H845 AUS) was sold to P&T Coaches in 1996, and influenced a change in livery. The chassis number was BDVVLM 093000, and it had a Deansgate body. It is still in daily service at the time of writing.*

Above: *D741 WRC was another purchase from James Watt & Son in 1996, and is a Ford R1014 (BCR SWP 408170) with a Plaxton Paramount I C45F body (8710FTP2C001) which was built in 1987. It was traded-in to Volvo at Loughborough in 1998 and went to T.R.S. of Leicester, but has just come back to Shetland at the time of writing.*

Left: *Outside the garage of P&T Coaches at Baltasound.*

Right: *Carrying a more modern white, yellow and blue livery, we see the latest addition to the P & T fleet. This Volvo B10M-48 (YV31MA518WA048172) with a Plaxton Premier 3200 C45F body (9710VMM7254) was acquired in 1998, when the company traded in D741 WRC. The picture is taken on the Esplanade at Lerwick, where R924 OPS is seen on tour work. When one considers the difference in vehicles between this coach and those that were working on Unst from 1950 onwards, it is important to note how much things have changed in just fifty years. As will be appreciated, with the exception of very small capacity vehicles, there was no bus service on the island until well after World War II. Today the village of Baltasound boasts one of the best kept bus shelters anywhere in the world!*

ROYAL AIR FORCE, SAXA VORD

The biggest employer on Unst in recent times has been the Royal Air Force, who opened its base on the island in 1955. This came about during the 'Cold War', at a time when Britain and her allies became increasingly concerned about the threat of Communist Russia. As preparations for national and civil defence increased, a number of military bases were opened to provide 'electronic capability', in other words bases that provided the country with an opportunity to see what the 'enemy' was up to, and whether or not any form of threat was evident.

Perhaps the most famous of these facilities was the RAF base at Fylingdale on the North Yorkshire Moors, but other 'secret' bases like Staxton Wold (Yorkshire) and Saxa Vord were equally important. In rural Essex a secret nuclear bunker was built with the capability to house 400 government officials and civil service personnel deep underground, but neither the locals nor the nation at large knew much about such places. High on the hill above Haroldswick construction work on RAF Saxa Vord began in the early-1950s, and before too long a radar dome dominated the prominent headland looking out towards the GIUK (Greenland-Iceland-UK) Gap. Through this area Russian shipping and aircraft gained access to the North Atlantic, and Saxa Vord was part of the facilities erected to keep an eye on these northern waters and the airspace above.

Despite the more relaxed climate in the years following the breakdown of the Iron Curtain, Saxa Vord has still maintained a role as part of the nation's defence system, and as such we are probably prohibited from talking much about it in a book like this. Even though the base has been considerably 'down-sized' in recent times, warning signs still exist to show a prohibition on taking photographs.

Throughout the years the RAF has operated a number of vehicles on Unst, many of which were concerned with the carriage of military personnel. These buses did not operate to normal scheduled services, but as they formed such an integral part of life on Unst for so many years, it would have been wrong to preclude them from this book.

Left: *The first 'service' bus on Unst was this Bedford SB with an unrecorded body. Although I dismantled this bus myself, I never thought to look for the builder's plate, but I think it would be either a Mulliner or a Marshall body. The vehicle is seen outside our old garage in Cullivoe at the end of the 1970s.*

Centre Left: *Photographed at Haroldswick, this bus is thought to be a Dodge, and is painted in the standard RAF olive green livery of that time. This scheme was later abandoned as it was considered to be too easily recognised by terrorists. This change followed a bomb attack on a military bus whilst it was crossing the M62 motorway near Hartshead in West Yorkshire.*

Bottom Left and Top Right: *A change in livery to bright, 'non-military' colours was considered to be the safest move, but the distinctive bodies built by Marshall of Cambridge, Reeve Burgess (and others) still made them a 'dead give-away'. Chassis at this time were generally Bedford or Dodge, but other makes were also used. Both these vehicles have been left on the island, and are now used for private 'domestic' purposes!*

Centre Right: *By the time we reached the 1990s, military buses began to look less identifiable, and more like the coaches in service with civilian operators. Many even took civilian registration plates like L416 GJO, which is a Dennis Javelin with a UVG body. The deep seats with plush moquette made the interiors something that the early servicemen at Saxa Vord would have difficulty in recognising as a 'service' bus.*

Below: *Apart from its military registration plate, one would be hard pressed to tell that JL 63 AA was an RAF coach. This Dennis Javelin carries another UVG body and is pictured inside the main part of the base in Haroldswick. All these coaches saw a variety of duties, ranging from the movement of men to the installation on top of the headland, to family shopping trips to Lerwick.*

The island of Yell is about 83 square miles with a population of around 1,000 and is an area considered to be the least fertile of all the inhabited islands; in all a large tract of heather and peat moorland. This is cut by deep voes at Whalefirth on the west and Bastavoe and Mid Yell on the east. It is also an area where I can talk about bus operations, since my grandfather started his coach business here back in 1922. It is a business that I have been around since I was a very small boy, as the picture right all too painfully shows. This was taken back in either 1951 or 1952, with a Bedford WLB outside our house at Moarfield.

R. G. JAMIESON & SON

Although this book is not particularly about our family fleet, my publisher has encouraged me to spend some time talking about this, in order to explain where my 'passion' in the subject stems from. To do that I must go back to 1922 when Robert Gordon Jamieson started his taxi and car hire business with a Model T Ford convertible. Registered PS 418, it was bought new for £250 in Edinburgh. Not only was this a very large sum of money in those days, but Edinburgh was also a very long way away and travel was not easy. I suspect he was either a man of vision or a bit of an adventurer, or possibly both! I think he would have had to be, for there were no metalled (tarmac) roads on Yell in those days, merely surfaces made up with hand-packed stones. Yet they did link one community with another, providing a route across the peat bogs and moorlands that make up much of the island surface. Indeed, many of the roads would remain little more than tracks until well after World War II, and some were still to be 'made up' in the early 1960s.

Hitherto much of the connection between villages on the island was by boat, and communication by water was as common then as it is by car now! When not out fishing, such boats would be seen providing services that linked island to island, and community to community. It was therefore something of a novelty when motor transport began. Of course there had long been overland travel, both on foot and by horse, and for many years an overland stagecoach service ran through Shetland linking the Mainland with the Northern Isles.

My grandfather had left Shetland during World War I to serve in the Merchant Navy, during which time he survived his ship (the SS *Queen Amelie*) being torpedoed by a German U-boat 25 miles north of Flugga. Quite why he turned to driving a car when he returned home, I can not really recall; however, like many people who went away from small rural communities during the war, he came back having seen a much wider world - a world in which the automobile and the internal combustion-engined commercial vehicle had begun to ascend. The family remained in crofting, and I suppose the car was just a side-line, but the business grew and he was operating four vehicles by 1930, including a new 7-seat Chevrolet bus. We remained with four vehicles all through World War II, and in 1948 we purchased our first big bus, the 20-seat Bedford shown above right.

This was very much our start into the coach business, and along with my cousin Robert Henry Jamieson we are still running the family coach and car hire business at the start of the 21st-Century. Over the years we have had 20 buses, coaches and mini-buses of 13-seats and above, plus a large number of cars and mini-buses with lower seating capacity. Our coaches were initially blue and cream, but we changed to blue and white in 1983. Our fleet list has included:-

Reg.	Chassis	Body	Cap.	Year	Acq.
RG 3561	Bedford WLB	Duple	C20F	1933	1948
LKJ 885	Austin K2-SL	Kenex	C17F	1949	New
CGE 200	Bedford ML	Duple	C14F	1939	1953
YJ 8939	Bedford OB	Plaxton	C27F	1947	1955
PS 1999	Bedford OB	Duple	B28F	1950	1960
PS 2001	Fordson Thames	Scottish Av	C29F	1950	1964
BJX 848C	Bedford VAS1	Duple	C29F	1965	1969
HPS 28P	Bedford YLQ	Duple	C45F	1976	New
KPS 600T	Bedford PJK	Plaxton	C29F	1978	New
RPS 380Y	Bedford YNT	Plaxton	C53F	1983	New
KGG 725Y	Mercedes 608D	Reeve Bur	C25F	1982	1985
E609 YPS	Mercedes 811D	Reeve Bur	C29F	1988	New
G250 CPS	Dennis	Plaxton	C53F	1989	New
D114 LSE	Bedford YNP	Plaxton	C35F	1987	1990
K294 ESF	Mercedes 814D	Plaxton	C33F	1993	1993
L456 HPS	Ford Transit	Ford	C14F	1993	New
H410 CJF	MAN 11.180	Caetano	C35F	1990	1994
P2 RGJ	Dennis	Plaxton	C57F	1997	New
T955 MBU	Ford Transit	Coachliner	C16F	1999	New

Also purchased by R.G. Jamieson & Son, but never operated in service:

630 CYS	Bedford C5C1	Duple	C29F	1961	1982
ex RAF	Bedford SB	Marshall(?)	(?)	(?)	1978
KWX 412	Bedford SB	Duple	C33F	1950/1	1978

Left: *Purchased brand new at a cost of around £1,700, this Austin K2-SL (131820) was bought direct from the Kenex factory at a time when commercial vehicles were very hard to come by. LKJ 885 had a 17-seat body, and was fitted out with red vinyl seats. It worked with us until 1961, when it was traded in against a new Austin Cambridge A55 MkII purchased from the Lerwick dealers Macleod and Maclean.*

Opposite Page Top: *A line up of coaches outside our garage at Cullivoe in 1955, with PS 2421 an 11-seat Morris Commercial, CGE 200 a 14-seat Bedford ML/Duple, LKJ 885 a 17-seat Austin/Kenex and YJ 8939 a 27-seat Bedford OB/Plaxton.*

Opposite Page Centre: *Our first big coach was this Bedford WLB (108911) with a 20-seat Duple body. Built in 1933, the WLB came to Yell from Leask's of Lerwick in 1948 for £800. It was taken out of service in 1953 when the body was broken up. However, with a home made platform the chassis, bonnet and cowl were converted into a truck for use on our croft.*

Below: *CGE 200 was a 1939 Bedford ML (12755) with a Duple 14-seat body (6044-2), and came direct to us from MacBrayne's in 1953. It came with the colourful MacBrayne livery, but it was repainted shortly afterwards. From the lack of an external radiator filler cap, it will be noted that this is one of the pre-war M-types, of which very few were made due to the outbreak of war in September 1939. The seating capacity in this vehicle was reduced due to a large mail/luggage box that MacBrayne's had fitted just inside the door. It was sold to a shop-keeper on Whalsay as spares for his travelling shop.*

Above: *Seen at the garage in Cullivoe, our next acquisition was the 1947 Bedford OB (33499), which was fitted with a Plaxton C27F body (206). It was bought from Hutcheson's of Dundee in 1955, and remained at work on Yell until 1972. YJ 8939 was then sold for use as a delivery van, but this never materialised; eventually Geoffrey Robertson converted it to a static fish and chip van at East Yell. It was later sold on for use as a peat shed, and was finally scrapped around 1995.*

Below: *The Austin and the Bedford OB await the arrival of the Tystie at Gutcher as it comes across the Bluemull Sound from Unst in or around 1957. Note the large number of passengers on the ferry!*

Left: *This is another view of the bus shown on our cover picture, and features PS 1999. It was a Bedford OB (141679) with a 28-seat Mulliner MkII service bus body (T563). It was built new for James Watt & Son, Reawick in 1950, and did 10 years service in Mainland before coming to Yell. As in the cover picture, the driver is my uncle James John Jamieson. He began driving for the firm when he was legally old enough, and is still taking passengers around the island. He has been known to most local school children, and has probably taken three generations to school at Mid Yell and Cullivoe. The picture is taken in the mid-1960s at the Sellafirth-Cunnister junction during road improvements. The OB lasted until 1968, when it was scrapped and the body used as a garden shed by James John - he had obviously become very attached to it!*

This Page: *We present two views of a well-known member of the Jamieson fleet which has now survived into preservation, indeed a picture of this vehicle is regularly used in an advert by the publishing company Ian Allan, as it endeavours to get people to subscribe to its bus magazines. Built in 1950, PS 2001 was a Fordson Thames ET6 (7238576) with a Scottish Aviation 29-seat body, that we purchased from Ganson Bros., of Lerwick in 1964. This was bought as an addition to the fleet and stayed in service until 1978, when it was stored in our garage. In 1982 it was sold into preservation with T.D. Heslop of Hexham, Northumberland. It has moved around over the subsequent years, but at the time of writing it is owned by Andrew Maiden in Wales.*

Right: *This, and all the other pictures on this page feature another member of our fleet that has now gone into preservation, Bedford VAS1 (2043) with a Duple Bella Vista 29-seat body (1184-45). This was our first diesel bus, which I bought for the company from SMT in Glasgow in October 1969. It was quite an adventure for a young man, who had been sent south to find a replacement for PS 1999, which had reached the end of its working days. Not only had I been given the responsibility to find a new bus or coach, but I also had the job of getting it back to Yell - no small task in the days before the ro-ro ferries. Indeed, as this picture confirms, its transportation gave me a few worrying moments. Here we see BJX 848C slung across the gunwales of* Shetlander, *an ex-fishing boat that had been converted to a supply vessel for the local council. We had brought BJX up to Lerwick on the deck of the* St. Clair, *but it then had to wait at Lerwick for a whole week until the weather improved sufficiently for the crossing of*

Yell Sound.

Right: *I so liked the colour scheme on BJX 848C, that I contemplated painting our other vehicles in a corresponding livery, and I repainted the coach in 1970. However, I eventually decided against re-painting all the other vehicles and changed the VAS into our traditional blue and cream in 1973, in which it is pictured outside the garage.*

Left: *When BJX 848C arrived at Cullivoe, it was painted in the livery of its first owners Abbeyways of Halifax. The scheme was buttermilk and primrose, and this had been retained when the coach was sold by Abbeyways at the age of just 13 months. The owner of Abbeyways at that time, Geoffrey Wainwright, found that he could actually make a good profit by just running a coach for one year, and selling it quickly on. Thus, as he was taking delivery of a vehicle, he would actually be ordering the next. In July 1966 BJX 848C went to South Wales, where it entered the service of George Warren in Neath. It is pictured here on the old bridge at the head of Bastavoe in 1970.*

Left: *Work for our VAS was quite demanding, and here we see it climbing out of Ulsta on the Overland Service during bad winter conditions in the mid-1970s. However, the little Bedford was no stranger to bad weather, having previously worked in both the South Pennines and the Welsh valleys. At one point on this journey the snow was actually higher than the top of the bus, so it was no easy task to take a fully loaded bus up such a steep climb.*

Right: *In 1981 a second livery style was applied, as we reversed the blue and the cream paint scheme. It remained in this livery until it was taken out of service at the end of 1984. It was then stored in our old garage at Cullivoe, with a view for eventual preservation. But here the vehicle slumbered for a total of 15 years before eventually being photographed by Philip Lamb, editor of* Preserved Bus *magazine. In March 2000, Mike Berry and Alan Earnshaw came up to Cullivoe, and between us we got the Bedford outside and running again. In June it moved down to Lerwick for the Ninth Shetland Classic Car Show, and then went to Appleby where it is now being*

Left: *When he reached 65, my grandfather passed on the business to my uncle Laurence G. Jamieson, and it is in his name that we see our next acquisition, HPS 28P - a Bedford YLQ (FW452929). Fitted with a Duple Dominant Express C45F body (616-2224), it is seen at the ferry terminal at Ulsta. It also sports a livery influenced by Premier Travel (Cambridge) that featured in Bedford publicity brochures of that time. The name L. G. Jamieson continued until 1979 when he died, at which time the business passed to his widow Belle. To ensure its continuation, the firm was bought by my cousin Robert Henry Jamieson and myself. The trading name then changed back to that of our grandfather Robert Gordon Jamieson & Son, but given the respective christian names of the two new proprietors the name was still very appropriate.*

Right: *In 1984 we repainted the Dominant, changing the cream portion of the livery to white. It is seen here at Symbister on Whalsay, with the harbour behind. This is the main base for fishing vessels in Shetland, and a vital part of the islands economy. The large vessels that operate from here land the catches at Lerwick, Scalloway and further afield, but the size of the vessels can be noted from the two big boats seen in the background of this picture.*

Left: *In 1997 the Dominant was completely refurbished and finished off in the same new three-tone blue metallic paint, that had been ordered for our new coach P2 RGJ, a Dennis Javelin with Plaxton body. This scheme would take our fleet into the 20th century, and it is still worn by HPS 28P as she remains in service today. The interior was also fully refurbished with brand new seats in a modern type of moquette, but in a design that was relevant to her original age.*

Right: *This was our next acquisition, and is seen at SMT Glasgow as part of the display for the Scottish Motor Show in 1978. The coach was KPS 600T, a Bedford PJK (HW450007) fitted with a Plaxton Supreme body (79PJK003) that provided 29 seats. After the show the coach was sent north to Shetland and entered service in November 1978, and was an addition to our fleet rather than a replacement. It became a jack of all trades, and enjoyed a wide variety of work.*

Left: *Taken outside our new 3-bay garage which had been built in 1976 to house the Dominant, we see the Bedford PJK just after delivery. It was to remain at work with us until 1983, when it was sold to the Shetland Island Council for work on Whalsay. As will be discussed later, the Bedford worked with the SIC for a number of years, until it was eventually bought for conversion to a mobile home for a band. However, during its conversion it was badly vandalised in Lerwick and ultimately scrapped.*

Right: *This Bedford YNT (DT102116) with a Plaxton Paramount 3200 MkI (8311NTP1C050) was new in 1983 to replace KPS 600T, and had 53 seats. It was the first coach to feature the two-tone blue colour scheme, although this was not yet a metallic paint. The round badge on the side of RPS 380Y was our Diamond Jubilee logo, marking 60 years of service. The picture is taken at West Sandwick in the winter of 1985 whilst on its way to collect school children coming home from Lerwick via the ferry to Ulsta. The Bedford remained with us until 1989 when it was sold to Semmence of Wynmondham (Norfolk), ahead of our purchase of G250 COS.*

Right: *A rear view of KGG 725Y taken on the road between West Sandwick and Mid Yell. Note that the vehicle carries our logo 'The Road To The Isles', which had been first applied to RPS 380Y in 1983, and still remains on all our larger coaches down to the present day.*

Left: *This Mercedes 608D (310427-20-546051) had a Reeve Burgess body conversion that provided 25 seats. It was built in 1982 and we purchased it in 1985 from Crainey of Kilsyth via the dealers Blythswood Motors in Glasgow. It remained with us until 1988 when KGG 725Y was sold back to Blythswood Motors, who later sold it on to Lewis Jones of Aberdare in Wales.*

Left: *Purchased to replace KGG 725Y, was E609 YPS a Mercedes 811D (670303-20-851692) with a Reeve Burgess 29-seat body (16914). It came new to our fleet in 1988, and remained with us for five years before eventually being sold to Shalder Coaches of Scalloway in 1993. Once again it is seen in the two-tone blue paint scheme outside our newer garage which was built to accommodate three coaches.*

Right: *This view is fairly typical of the type of roads on which our vehicles operate, and here we see E609 YPS heading toward Cullivoe from the north end of the island. Beyond this you can see the start of the open waters that head north towards the polar ice cap. To the north west would lay the Faroes and beyond that Iceland, to the east would be Norway, and the west Newfoundland, Canada and America. It will take little imagination to understand the gales that can sweep into Cullivoe during the winter months.*

Left (all three pictures): *This is G250 CPS, a Dennis Javelin (11SDA1906-494) with a Plaxton Paramount 3200 MkII 53-seat body (8911HEA1229), which we bought new in 1989. It was sold in 1997 to Windsorian of Berkshire via the dealers Kirkby of Anston. In its years with Jamieson's it got around quite a bit, and the top picture shows it at Maloy in Norway, then (centre) underneath the Eifel Tower in Paris, and finally (bottom) passing through snow drifts in Norway in July 1990.*

Above: *Next came this Bedford YMP (GT106189) with a Plaxton Paramount 3200 MkI body (868MQP2C013). This 35-seater was bought in 1990 from Collison of Stonehouse. This 1987 coach was with us until 1993, when D114 LSE was sold to Selwyn's of Runcorn, Cheshire. It later worked at Manchester Airport, where it became known as the* Shetland

Above & Below: *This Mercedes 814D (670313-2N-003750) had a Plaxton Beaver 33-seat body (928.5MMYO611); it was purchased at the age of just three months in June 1993, and sold in November 1993 to Porteous of Anlaby (Alpha Coaches, Hull). Despite its short time in Yell, K294 ESF still travelled some distance including a trip to Norway, where it is pictured at Kristiansand. Note the giant teapot, and Gulliver laying on the hillside beyond. The coach was never repainted in our colours, and retained the Sproat livery.*

Left: *In our work on Yell, it is obvious that we need small capacity vehicles for a variety of duties, and over the years we owned and operated a range of mini-buses. Obviously, those with less than 13-seats do not form part of this book, but the larger capacity mini-buses do. The first mini-bus that we acquired within this range was this Ford Transit (BDVEPC97584), which had a 14-seat Ford conversion body. It was new in 1993, and carried the registration number L456 HPS, and was painted in a three-tone blue and white livery as shown in this illustration.*

Right: *In 1997 we changed the livery to a two-tone blue and white livery and added a gold stripe along the sides. The large vinyl lettering was retained from the original colour scheme, as were the RGJ initials on the bonnet. The vehicle is still at work in our fleet, and at the time of writing is accompanied by another three mini-buses, these are an 8-seat Transit (S146 JPS), a 16-seat Transit Long Cube (T955 MBU) and a new14-seat Transit (W471 GPS).*

Right: *Our most recent big coach was P2 RGJ, which came new in 1997. It was purchased to replace our Dennis Javelin G250 CPS as a means of up-dating the fleet and also moving up to the 12-metre range. Once again we chose the Dennis Javelin (1250A2155-1265) and had another Plaxton body. This time we bought the Premier 3200 (9512HBM3896) via the dealers Kirkby of Anston. It had 57 seats, but we reduced this to 53 in order to provide more leg room for our passengers. It too has travelled all over northern Europe, but is seen here at Edinburgh Castle in 1999.*

Left: *Another member of the current fleet is our MAN 10.180 (HOCL-R4690419G056110) fitted with a 35-seat Caetano Algarve I body (958052). Registered H410 CJF it was new to Ralph of Langley, and purchased by ourselves in March 1994 to replace K294 ESF. The coach has a low driving position, and I have taken it on some lengthy journeys from Yell, including Denmark, Norway, Holland, Ireland, and to many distant places in mainland Scotland and England.*

Left: *The last vehicle to be purchased in the 20th-century was T955 MBU, a long wheel base Ford Transit 190 Turbo-Diesel (BDVLXCO5605). It has a Coachliner conversion to the body, and is fitted with 16 proper coach seats. Internally it is trimmed just like our big coaches, so that passengers can still be carried in comfort when the run does not warrant using one of our larger vehicles. Of course this is not the most modern vehicle in the fleet, but all the other acquisitions have come after our 31st December 1999 cut off date. As a result this picture shows the Transit before the lining out is added. We are always willing to provide coaches, mini-buses, taxis and self drive cars, and (here is my advert) we can be contacted on 01957 744214!*

THE TRUSTEES OF T. R. MANSON

This firm was based at West Sandwick, Yell, and commenced just after World War I, when T.R. Manson purchased what may have been a Model T Ford for taxi work on the island. When he died the business was left to his wife, and after his death the company was continued by trustees acting on her behalf. The firm's first large bus was purchased new in 1946, when an 18-seat Austin was acquired. The livery was initially maroon and cream, but two later acquisitions ran in the tan and cream of the former owners (Thomson of Sandwick) and were never repainted. When the firm purchased a Bedford SB from Johnson's of Scalloway in 1968, all the remaining vehicles were repainted into the blue and cream to match the SB. The firm was eventually sold to Hugh Sinclair & Co. in 1971, with the vehicles FBU 493, ERG 164 and KWX 412 being taken over.

Reg.	Chassis	Body	Cap.	Year	Acq.
PS 1385	Austin	Croft	B18F	1946	New
AGS 676	Bedford MLZ	SMT	B19F	1944	1950
BKS 179	Bedford OB	Mulliner	B27F	1950	1952
FBU 493	Bedford OB	Duple	C29F	1949	1958
ERG 164	Bedford OB	Duple	C29F	1950	1961
KWX 412	Bedford SB	Duple	C33F	1950/1	1968

Above: *Seen at the Ulsta ferry terminal with the Shalder arriving from Toft, are two vehicles from the fleet of The Trustees of T.R. Manson. Awaiting the passengers on the left is BKS 179 a Bedford OB with a Mulliner body, whilst on the right is AGS 676 a Bedford MLZ with a SMT body.*

Centre Right: *This Austin (85690) has an 18-seat Croft body. Registered PS 1385 it arrived new in 1946 and was scrapped on the island in 1961.*

Bottom Right: *AGS 676 Bedford MLZ (28606) had a 19-seat SMT body and was built in 1944. It came to Yell in 1950 from the Loch Katrine Steam Boat Co. Callander. Withdrawn in 1966 it was sold to Norman Tulloch of Awick for a store shed.*

Left: *The third vehicle in the Manson fleet was BKS 179, a Mulliner-bodied (T500) 27-seat Bedford OB (117160), which dated from 1950. It arrived on Yell in 1952 having been purchased from W. Thomson of Sandwick. It was never re-painted and ran in the colours of Thomson until it was sold in 1960 to J. G. Hunter & Son of Unst. It had a service bus specification, but it also had luggage racks which were extremely useful for passengers on the Overland Service. It is on this working that BKS 179 is seen at Ulsta in the mid-1950s.*

Below (both): *The next acquisition came from Redwing Tours of North Shields (Northumberland) in 1958. This was a 1949 Bedford OB (114825) with a Duple Vista C29F body (54366). Registered FBU 493, it was painted in a cream and maroon livery and stayed like this until they were all re-painted in 1968. The lower picture taken at Scatlands, West Sandwick shows the OB with driver Lell Robertson of the Herra, who drove with this firm for many years. When the firm was sold in 1970, FBU 493 was one of the vehicles that passed to Hugh Sinclair & Co., also of West Sandwick .*

Above and Below: *Another acquisition from Thomson of Sandwick, was a 1950 OB (145540) with a Duple Vista C29F body (56575). It was the only Shetland OB to be fitted with roof cant rail windows. For a while ERG 164 retained the Thomson tan-colour after purchase in 1961, but was eventually repainted blue and cream (as seen below) when KWX 412 arrived.*

Below: *A view of Bedford SB (3743) with a Duple Vega body (56794) KWX 412, which was new in 1950 and registered in August 1951. The 33-seat Big Bedford is seen on the pier at Gutcher, some time after it moved to Yell from Johnson's of Scalloway. It was sold to me for preservation in 1980, and is currently waiting to go south for complete restoration.*

HUGH SINCLAIR & CO.

The transport operation at West Sandwick had two distinct sides, with the coaches being operated by the Trustees of T. R. Manson and the taxi business by the firm of Hugh Sinclair, although they both worked from the same garage under one basic management. When the widow of T. R. Manson died in 1971, the business was taken over by Andrew Williamson. The three Bedford coaches shown above - namely the SB (KWX 412), and two OBs (ERG 164 and FBU 493) were the basis for the new company fleet. It is still trading today, and over the years has served the residents and schoolchildren of West Sandwick with the following fleet:-

Reg.	Chassis	Body	Cap.	Year	Acq.
FBU 493	Bedford OB	Duple	C29F	1949	1971
ERG 164	Bedford OB	Duple	C29F	1950	1971
KWX 412	Bedford SB	Duple	C33F	1950/1	1971
WGD 551	Bedford SB3	Duple	C41F	1959	1976
JSN 178L	Leyland	Maclay	C20F	1973	1977
6876 SM	Bedford SB3	Plaxton	C41F	1962	1979
TLS 286P	Bedford NJM	Plaxton	C41F	1976	1980
PGB 870V	Bedford CFL	Reebur	C17F	1980	New
C331 FSU	Dodge S-56	Reeve	C25F	1985	New
D428 MHS	Freight Rover	Scott	C16F	1986	New
G101 CSF	Mercedes 811D	Alexander	C33F	1989	New
L254 VSU	Mercedes 709D	Dormobile	C29F	1993	New
P158 NVM	LDV	-	C16F	1997	New

Top: *Line up of the acquired buses at West Sandwick c1971.*

Centre Right: *ERG 164 and KWX 412 at Ulsta pier.*

Bottom Right: *The first 'new' vehicle acquired by Sinclair was WGD 551, a Bedford SB3 (68733) with a Duple Super Vega II body (1105-304) which came to Yell at the age of 17 years. It remained in service until 1979 when it became a greenhouse alongside a house in West Sandwick.*

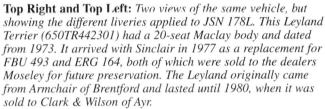

Top Right and Top Left: *Two views of the same vehicle, but showing the different liveries applied to JSN 178L. This Leyland Terrier (650TR442301) had a 20-seat Maclay body and dated from 1973. It arrived with Sinclair in 1977 as a replacement for FBU 493 and ERG 164, both of which were sold to the dealers Moseley for future preservation. The Leyland originally came from Armchair of Brentford and lasted until 1980, when it was sold to Clark & Wilson of Ayr.*

Centre Right Top: *This Bedford SB3(89150) with a Plaxton Embassy C41F body (G22897) was registered in 1962 with the number 6876 SM and came to Shetland to work with Leask's of Lerwick in 1966 (it is in their livery that it was photographed, but as it ran in these colours with Hugh Sinclair this is still appropriate). It arrived in West Sandwick in 1979 and remained in service until 1980, at which time it was scrapped and the body was sold for use as a shed in West Yell.*

Centre Right Bottom: *This Bedford NJM (EW458261) was fitted with a Plaxton Supreme body (76NJM004) with 41 seats. Registered TLS 286P it was new in 1976, and was acquired from Campbell of Clydebank in 1980. It was sold on to Cliff Whitney of Cullivoe for use as a horsebox, but it was never converted to this purpose and was re-sold to Allan & Black, Arboyne in March 1992.*

Below: *This unique 1976 photograph shows a line up of five different Bedford-Duple coaches that were being operated on Yell at the same time. Running from left to right, and showing the vehicles in descending age we have:-*
Jamieson's Bedford YLQ-Duple Dominant, Jamieson's Bedford VAS-Duple Bella Vista, then Sinclair's Bedford SB3-Duple Super Vega II, and Bedford SB-Duple Vega, and finally their Bedford OB-Duple Vista (with cant rail roof lights). From newest to oldest, there was a 26 year difference in the age range.

Top Left: *This Bedford CFL (JY631642) is a development of the Bedford CF light commercial chassis, which began life as a 15-cwt van. By the early 1980s, the long wheel base variants were being used for some amazing applications, including this bus body by Reeve Burgess (12613) which carried 17 passengers. PGB 870V was bought new in 1980 and sold on to Logans in Ballymena, Northern Ireland in 1985.*

Top Right: *Next came this Dodge S-56 (FD213712) which had a Reeve Burgess C25F body (15286) and was ordered new in 1985. It was withdrawn in 1994, but C331 FSU is still standing in the garage at West Sandwick at the time of writing.*

Centre Left Top: *A change to British Leyland-Rover came in 1986, when Sinclair's purchased this smart looking Freight Rover 350D (JA266966) with a Scott body conversion. This was a development of the old British Leyland Sherpa van, but it had seen considerable improvement by the time this Freight-Rover was produced. The Scott conversion on D428 MHS provided 16 seats, which is seen here at the Gutcher Ferry Terminal. It was sold for conversion back to a van in 1997.*

Centre Left Bottom: *G101 CSF is a Mercedes 811D (670303-20-935473) fitted with an Alexander C35F body (AM60-288-12). New in 1989, it is still operating today.*

Bottom Left: *Another Mercedes (L254 VSU) joined the fleet in 1993, when this new 709D (669003-2N-016535) was purchased with a Dormobile C29F body (5266263393). It is also still working with the firm today.*

Bottom Right: *The final addition to the fleet (in 1997) was another mini bus development from the old Sherpa van range. This time the vehicle is the LDV long wheel base model (SYEZMNFFEDN017317), which has been converted to provide 16 seats, although there is no indication on the vehicle of the firm that carried out this work. However, P158 NVM is well-appointed internally with comfortable coach seats.*

H.R. WILLIAMSON

This small operator established a business at Sellafirth, Yell in 1949, when he acquired his solitary bus. This was a Bedford WLB (109536) with a Duple 29-seat body which had been built in 1934. It was registered GS 4634, and had been acquired second-hand from Alexander (western) where it was fleet no. W228, at a time when this operator was disposing with their old WL and WH series Bedfords as the new OB-Types became available after World War II.

Williamson only operated for about a year, having enjoyed only a limited amount of private hire work and no services. On the demise of the business the old Bedford was sold on to J. W. Laurenson on Unst, and became his first vehicle - the subsequent history of which has already been told. The Bedford is photographed here at Ulsta, when it arrived from the south in 1949. It is seen set across the gunwales, whilst the inset picture shows the side elevation of the Duple body.

A. K. ANDERSON

Another one-bus operator that existed on Yell for a very short period of time, was the firm of A. K. Anderson of Mid-Yell. Anderson's was an established truck operation, started by Gibbie (Gilbert) F. Anderson. His son eventually took over the business and he decided to have a go in the coaching business,. In 1956 he bought a Bedford OWB (23908) with a SMT Utility body, which was one of the 'relaxed' models that had been built in 1945. It came from Ganson Bros. of Lerwick, who had improved the seating in the bus, so it was more of a coach than the service bus B28F specification recorded. The only known photograph of it on Yell shows it in the picture of Jessamine Clark (with her sister Emma as the bridesmaid) on the day of her wedding to Ian Nisbet on 28th July1960.

As will be seen from the clarity of this colour picture, the bus retained the grey, cream and red livery of Ganson Bros. The inset illustration shows the road tax licence for EFS 183 in 1959. Once this operation came to an end, the OWB was sold off for use as a workman's caravan before being finally scrapped.

R. ROBERTSON & SON

The final operator to be covered in the chapter on Yell is the firm started by Robbie (Robert) Robertson, from Ulsta. Under the name of R. Robertson & Son, the family still operate the local shop and a taxi business. For many visitors to Yell, this is the first place to visit when they get off the boat after crossing Yell Sound. Having operated taxis and small mini-buses over the years, Tommy Robertson (the son of the founder) got a contract to carry local school children. To do this work they obtained WRN 802V, a new Ford Transit (BDVPWJ428890) with a 16-seat Dormobile body (3746) in 1980. After losing the contract in 1983, it was sold to Shalder Coaches in 1984. In 1999 a second large mini-bus (P934 CBV) was acquired from S. D. Beachmore plc of Wigan. This is seen in the bottom picture, which shows a 1997 LDV Convoy (SEYZMYSEEDNO16656), with a 16-seat body. It was purchased when a second school contract was obtained, and it is still working from Ulsta.

The next area to be considered is the North Mainland, a part of the Mainland which is almost an island in its own right. Connected to the Mainland by a narrow spit of land at Mavis Grind, it is surrounded by the North Sea on the east and the Atlantic on the west. The main settlements are Hillswick, Ollaberry, Eshaness and North Roe.

A. RATTER

Based at Ollaberry, Arthur Ratter just had one bus (seen above), which he used on an infrequent service to Lerwick. He operated this service between 1942 and 1945, with a Chevrolet (U65407) with an unknown body. It carried 14 passengers and had been purchased from P. J. Smith of Sandwick. In 1945 it was sold to J. Peterson of Ollaberry, who continued as follows:

J. PETERSON

Joseph Peterson (better known as Josie) was also based in Ollaberry and ran services from Hillswick and Eshaness that connected with the service to Lerwick. The vehicles were always painted blue and cream, and this continued until 1966 when he retired and sold the business to one of his drivers, Harry Wood.

Reg.	Chassis	Body	Cap.	Year	Acq.
SC 7513	Chevrolet	?	B14F	1930	1945
CNB 752	Bedford WHB	Duple (?)	B14F	1936	1946
WG 8476	Bedford WTB	Duple	C14F	1939	1946
AMS 339	Bedford OWB	SMT	B28F	1945	1946
PS 1991	Bedford OB	Mulliner	B28F	1950	New
BCB 96	Bedford OB	Plaxton	C30F	1948	1952
KWX 440	Bedford SB	Duple	C33F	1951	1959
399 ETB	Bedford SB3	Duple	C41F	1956	1962

Top: *This Chevrolet (SC 7513) was operated initially in the Northern Mainland by A. Ratter and was then taken over by J. Peterson. It was sold in 1946 to James Watt & Son.*

Centre Left: *This 1936 Bedford WHB (CNB 752) with a Duple body was obtained in 1946, and sold to J. C. Mowat of Eshaness on an unrecorded date.*

Bottom Left: *The third member of the Peterson fleet was this 1946 Bedford OWB (24683) with a SMT Utility 28-seat body. Registered AMS 339, it was originally operated by Alexander's as fleet number W187. It is seen (with its front end cropped off) in this photograph of the Peterson bus stand outside the Thule Bar in Lerwick during the 1950s.*

Above: *A wonderful colour picture of Bedford O-Types headed by PS 1991, Peterson's OB (138294) with a Mulliner B28F body (T560). It is parked near the Esplanade, with the Malakoff boatyard behind. The red O-Type is an ESSO Petroleum tanker followed by another O-Type lorry, this time one belonging to James Johnson & Son, Scalloway, which is probably fetching fish. This OB was actually the fifth member of the Peterson fleet, but has been shown slightly out of sequence in order to present this shot in a larger picture frame.*

Centre Right Top: *The fourth bus purchased by Peterson was a Bedford WTB (15822) with a Duple C14F body . We have no record of the body number, but its registration plate was WG 8476. It was acquired as a 10-year old vehicle from Beaton's of Portree on the Isle of Skye, and remained in service until 1959 when it was scrapped.*

Centre Right Bottom: *Plaxton coaches were not all that common in Shetland, but this is a forward-control Bedford OB (58000) with a full-front Plaxton C30F body (320). No pictures of BCB 96 are known in the Peterson livery, so it is shown when owned by J J & A Leslie of Sumburgh. The picture is taken at the upper bus station Lerwick.*

Bottom Left: *As will have been noted before in this narrative, an early Bedford SB, KWX 412 was operated in Shetland from 1955 onwards. This coach had been a Vauxhall demonstrator and was driven on trade plates. It was registered in the West Riding of Yorkshire in August 1951, when it was sold to Kildare of East Ardwick. A similar registered SB (3370) with a Duple Vega body (1006/256) was KWX 440, which was new to Balme of Otley in August 1951. It was purchased by Peterson in 1959 and is seen here in the lower bus park at Lerwick.*

Bottom Right: *This Bedford SB3 (60893) with Duple Super Vega C41F body (1090/247), registered 399 ETB, is seen leaving Lerwick at approximately 5pm on the service to Ollaberry.*

H. WOOD

As stated previously, Harry Wood was a driver with Peterson's of Ollaberry, and he took over the operation in 1966. However, a change of operating base eventually took place, and the company relocated to Wood's home village of North Roe. As far as I can recall, the Peterson livery was retained on the three vehicles he took over, but when he acquired his only purchase, a Bedford VAS5, it came in a black and white colour scheme,. This livery was retained on this coach until the business was sold to Robert A. Smith in 1976.

Reg.	Chassis	Body	Cap.	Year	Acq.
PS 1991	Bedford OB	Mulliner	B28F	1950	1966
KWX 440	Bedford SB	Duple	C33F	1951	1966
339 ETB	Bedford SB3	Duple	C41F	1956	1966
HXG 370F	Bedford VAS5	Duple	C29F	1968	1974

Top Left: *A further view of PS 1991 parked in the lower Lerwick bus park, still wearing the Peterson livery; however, as this livery was retained by Harry Wood after the take-over, it is entirely appropriate to show it here. As will be appreciated, it is taken in the lower section of the bus station in Lerwick which was predominantly used by operators from the north mainland, whilst the south mainland operators used the top part. This coach was sold to T.A. Arthur on Whalsay in 1970.*

Centre Left Top: *Again carrying Peterson's blue and cream livery, we present a view of the 'Big Bedford' SB (KWX 440), with its 3-litre petrol engine on Victoria pier. This was one of a number of such vehicles to work in Shetland, and is seen here in Lerwick awaiting a departure for the North Mainland.*

Centre Left Bottom: *With its distinctive 'butterfly grill' we see the 1956-built Duple Super Vega (399 ETB) at the departure point in Hillswick. The SB3 chassis on which the coach was built was a development of the 'Big Bedford' whilst the Duple Super Vega was a progression from the Duple Vega model shown above. It was sold to A. J. Eunson in 1974.*

Bottom Left: *The only 'new' coach purchased from outside Shetland was HXG 307F, a Bedford VAS5 (TT452932) with a Duple Bella Vista C29F body (1217/20) dating from 1968. It was acquired from Newton of Dingwall in 1976, and is seen here in Lerwick bus park. Like ETB 399, it passed to Bob Smith when the business was sold in 1976.*

R. A. SMITH

In 1976 a new name appears in our account, for this was when R. A. (Bob) Smith acquired the Wood operation, taking over two members of the fleet. Two years later he bought DTO 15C, in a brown and cream livery, resulting in a multi-coloured fleet. Of his three vehicles, each had a different livery; 399 ETB retained it's Peterson blue and cream paintwork, HGX 307F was the black and white of Woods, and DTO 15C was the third colour scheme.

Actually this Bedford SB5 with a Plaxton Panorama body, was called the *Lucinda Rose*. The idea for this came from a similar vehicle owned by Pat Isbister (of Walls) who, at that time, operated the SB5 registered FWT 322C. This vehicle had arrived in Shetland bearing the name *Princess Rose*, and Bob Smith so liked the name that he adopted a similar one for his coach, but called it after his wife Lucinda. By 1980 the business had been sold to Shalder Coaches along with 399 ETB, and Smith moved south with both his remaining buses, effectively using them as removal vehicles to transfer his household possessions.

Reg.	Chassis	Body	Cap.	Year	Acq.
339 ETB	Bedford SB3	Duple	C41F	1956	1976
HXG 370F	Bedford VAS5	Duple	C29F	1968	1976
DTO 15C	Bedford SB5	Plaxton	C41F	1965	1978

Top: *This photograph of DTO 15C taken in Lerwick bus station is slightly out of sequence, as this was actually the last bus to be purchased by Smith. The SB5 (96896) with its Plaxton Panorama 41-seat body (653137) came from Leamland of Uckfield in 1978, and left Shetland with its owner two years later.*

Centre Right: *A further view of 399 ETB taken in the bus station in Lerwick.*

Bottom Right: *Here we see HXG 307F followed by James Watt's OJH 128D at the Brig o'Fitch outside Lerwick (by the Scalloway junction) on their way home with the 5pm service.*

Brae is the third largest town in Shetland, located south of the isthmus at Mavis Grind which connects The Mainland with North Mainland. It is also near Sullom Voe, which has considerably aided local prosperity since the opening of the huge oil terminal there.

JOHN HAY

The business of John Hay seems to have been commenced at North Brae during World War I, when a Ford (Model T?) was used as a hiring car. This was followed by a further Ford and then a Commer, which could convert from a bus to a goods van. It may have been registered PS 1041 and possibly dated from 1933-4. The business was then taken over by his son, also called John Hay, and in 1941 Hay purchased another Commer, this time a 10-year old Invader (28223) with a Walker 'Comfort Coach' 20-seat body. Registered RG 2186 it came from Tait of Lerwick, and was painted in a mottled finish as seen in the picture at the head of this page. I know very little about the operation by John Hay, as this took place during the war years, but it seems that a service was offered from Brae to Lerwick, running via Muckle Roe on Tuesdays and Thursdays, and via Mossbank on Saturdays. He sold business and coach to C. Hawick of Brae who was later joined by A. Williamson. Between them they scrapped RG 2186 and bought EFS 176 and later sold it to A Jamieson, Voe.

R. A. SANDISON (left)

We now turn to another small operator in the Brae area, namely R. A. Sandison of Hillswick. Sandison was based at Hillswick and operated tourist services from the local hotel, although it appears to have been little used and possibly only run during the summer months. The tourists were carried around the area in a former MacBrayne's Morris Commercial. It may well have been a relatively unprofitable business because throughout its life the Morris retained the MacBrayne livery. Indeed, as the photograph opposite shows, little was done to disguise its former identity. The word 'MacBrayne' was painted out as was 'Mail' from Royal Mail Service resulting in a decrepit looking bus with the grandiose title of 'Royal Service' painted on the side.

The vehicle was last licensed in 1937 and obviously the service had petered out by the time the war broke out in 1939. As a consequence the vehicle stood semi-derelict for many years and the body was eventually purchased by P. J. Smith of Sandwick. He refurbished the body and fitted it to a former Bedford army lorry complete with the military style tin front. This has already been discussed in the paragraph dealing with Unst where the body ended its days although it will later be discussed under the operation of Smith's of Sandwick.

C. HAWICK (HAWICK & WILLIAMSON)

The business of John Hay was taken over by Christie Hawick who was joined in the operation by A.Williamson in 1948. The business then became known as Hawick & Williamson, and was also based at Brae. Hawick took over the Commer Invader with a Walker body (Comfort Coach) that had been operated by Hay and also continued the thrice-weekly service into Lerwick. In 1949 the Comfort Coach was scrapped and replaced with a Bedford OWB (23676), with a SMT Utility 32-seat body, which was purchased from SMT. (Both vehicles are pictured on Page 34.) Operations with the OWB seem to have been very very short and in 1950 the vehicle was sold to A. W. Jamieson of Voe.

Reg.	Chassis	Body	Cap.	Year	Acq.
RG 2186	Commer Invader	Walker	C20F	1931	1946
EPS 176	Bedford OWB	SMT	B32F	1944	1949

A. JAMIESON

The business of Hawick & Williamson passed to Arthur Jamieson, who was better known locally as Ertie. Jamieson, from the village of Voe, continued the same type of service as before, by running three times a week into Lerwick. Few pictures have been preserved from this period but top right we show his OWB with a picture of Jamieson and a young boy. The inset picture shows Ertie resting on the front bumper of the maroon and cream OWB with the registration number clearly visible behind. Jamieson continued to run the business until 1956 when it was passed to Manson Bros. of Brae.

MANSON BROS

As noted above Manson's took possession of the OWB EFS 176 and took over the services that Jamieson had formerly operated into Lerwick. By 1961 the OWB was getting a little long in the tooth and Manson's got a Bedford OB with a SMT body, which they had purchased from Georgeson & Moore of Scalloway. The OWB lasted for three more years and was finally scrapped in 1964. The OB also ran until 1964 but it was then sold to Johnson Bros. of Brae along with the business.

Reg.	Chassis	Body	Cap.	Year	Acq.
EFS 176	Bedford OWB	SMT	B32F	1944	1956
GTV	Bedford OWB	Duple	B28F	1944	1958
PS 1407	Bedford OB	SMT	C29F	1946	1961

Below: *Manson's Bedford OB (15088) with a SMT C29F body, registered PS 1407. Seen in the lower bus park at Lerwick, this coach was purchased from Georgeson & Moore in 1961 and sold three years later to Johnson Bros. of Brae.*

Above: *This provides another view of the SMT Utility-bodied Duple OWB (EFS 176) in service with Manson Bros. It's working life was extended when GTV 597 (a Duple-bodied OWB) was purchased for spares from Georgeson & Moore in 1958 . The SMT-bodied coach was probably withdrawn when the OB was bought in 1961 but it was only scrapped when the business came to an end in 1964.*

JOHNSON BROTHERS

As noted overleaf the business of Manson Bros. passed to the Johnson Brothers of Brae in 1964. The two brothers Harold and John were based at Bayview. Initially this was a one-bus business but at various times the brothers owned two or three vehicles at a given date. The new firm continued the Brae - Lerwick service that had begun with John Hay, but this run was supplemented by the transport of school children and occasional private hire work. After almost twenty years of doing this business the brothers sold out to Bolts Coaches of Lerwick in 1983, at which time Bolts opened a depot in Brae; details of the Bolts operation will be discussed in the section covering the South Mainland even though the firm also had a depot in Lerwick for some time.

Above: *Acquired from Manson Bros at the time of purchasing the business, the Bedford OB - SMT 29-seat coach was the first vehicle in the Johnson fleet. However PS 1407 was some 18-years old at the time of acquisition, and it would last little more than a year before being replaced by a more utilitarian Bedford. It is seen here about to depart from Lerwick with the service to Brae during Johnson's ownership and thus wearing their livery of blue and grey. This can only have been taken a few months before it was scrapped in 1965.*

Centre Right: *What replaced the OB was this Bedford SBG (33377) with a Mulliner B36F body registered NGY 823. As will be observed it had a 'military' specification body, and its austere appointments can hardly have been the most conducive for passengers travelling between Brae and Lerwick. Purchased from Dunnet of Keiss in 1965 it is seen parked outside the garage at Brae; it was scrapped in 1974.*

Bottom Right: *An attractive Burlingham Seagull C35F body (6307) on a Bedford SBG (47108) chassis. Dating from 1955 HMS 227 was purchased from John Leask & Son in May 1974 to replace NGY 823, and scrapped five years later.*

The fleet list for Johnson Brothers, was as follows

Reg.	Chassis	Body	Cap.	Year	Acq.
PS 1407	Bedford OB	SMT	C29F	1946	1964
NGY 823	Bedford SBG	Mulliner	B36F	1955	1965
HMS 227	Bedford SBG	Burlingham	C35F	1955	1974
LSN 56	Bedford SB3	Duple	C41F	1960	1978
GRS 12E	Leyland Cub	Alexander	B43D	1967	1980
PGM 641H	Bedford VAM70	Duple	C45F	1970	1981
GRS 11E	Leyland Cub	Alexander	B43D	1967	1982

Top Right: *Johnson's were to purchase three vehicles from John Leask & Son over the years, the second of which was LSN 56. This coach was new in 1960, and was comprised of a Bedford SB3 chassis (75428) and a Duple Super Vega II C41F body (1120/283). It came to Johnson in March 1978, but it was already 18-years old by this time. It lasted until the end of the operation in 1983, but it probably stood out of use for some time before the business was sold to Bolts Coaches in 1983; it then went south for preservation, but I have no idea what has happened to it since.*

Centre Right Top: *In March 1980 an odd coincidence began to occur when Johnson's purchased GRS 12E from the Kirkwall firm Peace's. The Alexander-bodied (72/71-156-6/6) Leyland Cub (PSUC1/13750670) had dual doors and a seating capacity for 43 passengers, and had originally been owned by Grampian; at this time it's sister bus GRS 11E was in service with John Leask & Sons in Lerwick, and the two would often be seen side by side in the town.*

Centre Right Bottom: *As will be appreciated, the Johnson Brothers fleet was never well-endowed with modern vehicles, but at a mere 11-years old, PGM 641H became the firm's youngest acquisition when it was purchased from Shalder Coaches in April 1981. This Bedford VAM70 (OT478366) had a Duple Viceroy 45-seat body, and is seen at the firm's Brae garage.*

Below: *Although no photographs of GRS 11E have been found in the Johnson livery, we see it here in service with Leask's at Lerwick. This vehicle (chassis no. PSUC1/13750669) joined the Brae-based firm in April 1982, and thus completed the coincidence. It was then re-united with its former stablemate until the business was finally sold to Bolts in 1983.*

J.F. JOHNSON & SON

Based in the garage formally occupied by Johnson Bros, one could expect that a firm started by John F. Johnson (better known as Jackie) might have some family connection with the earlier Brae bus operators. However, J. F. Johnson & Son (trading as Johnson Transport) has no direct family connection with Johnson Brothers. Jackie began in 1950, and the firm was later passed down to his son Gary who entered the bus business in 1991. Working mostly with mini buses, he purchased his first 24 seat midi bus in 1997 when a Mercedes with a PMT body was added to the fleet. In 1999 a brand new 29-seat Mercedes was bought to meet the specifications for modern public service vehicles and includes disabled facility access. Gary still operates his business from Brae doing mostly school work along with feeder services to the public services operated by John White. The fleet today numbers around nine vehicles, and at the time of writing has just been supplemented with the firm's first full-sized coach.

Reg.	Chassis	Body	Cap.	Year	Acq.
E824 HSN	Ford Transit	Ford	C14F	1987	1991
H801 TSA	Ford Transit	Ford	C14F	1990	1993
K546 OGA	Ford Transit	Deansgate	C15F	1993	1994
H854 YSP	Ford Transit	Ford	C14F	1990	1996
L330 KSS	Ford Transit	Ford	C14F	1993	1996
E463 YDM	Mercedes 609D	PMT	C24F	1987	1997
R132 VHJ	Ford Transit	Ford	C14F	1998	1998
S710 KSA	Ford Transit	Ford	C16F	1998	New
T500 APS	Mercedes 0814D	Plaxton	B29F	1999	New
P249 VEH	Ford Transit	Ford	C14F	1997	1999
P380 CBV	Ford Transit	Ford	C14F	1996	1999

Above: *A picture of the Johnson fleet seen at Mavis Grind, near Brae in 1999. This well-known beauty spot is a good setting to show off the Mercedes and the seven Ford Transit mini buses. Quite close to the point where this picture was taken, you can stand on a beach at the edge of the North Sea. If you were to pick up a stone at this point, then turn 180 degrees, it is possible to throw the stone into the Atlantic Ocean! I know that this has nothing to do with Shetland buses, but it is one of the many unique aspects of Shetland life and lore.*

Centre Left Top: *Gary Johnson's first mini bus was E824 HSN, a Transit (BADVVHT98747) with 14-seats. It was purchased from the Shetland Islands Council (SIC) at Lerwick, and was later sold, but I have no disposal date for this.*

Centre Left Bottom: *Second (from Harpers of Aberdeen) came Ford Transit H801 TSA (BDV2LM08935).*

Bottom Left: *The third mini bus was Ford Transit (BDVLMU 85323) K546 0GA, which was purchased with a Deansgate body from Muir of Coalburn in September 1994 and sold to the SIC to work on Whalsay in 1997.*

Above: *Ford Transit H854 YSP (BDVLMU85323) with a Ford conversion body, purchased from the SIC in August 1996.*

Above: *This 1993 Transit L330 KSS (BDVEPR88887) came from Harper Self Drive in 1996 and is now used at Sullom Voe.*

Above: *This Mercedes 609D with a 24-seat PMT body, E463 YDM, was swapped with the SIC for K546 0GA.*

Above: *Yet another Ford Transit (BDVEVR67321) with a 14-seat body was a 1998 demonstrator purchased in July 1998.*

Above: *With chassis number BDVLWT39032, S710 KSA carries 16 passengers and was new in October 1998.*

Above: *This Mercedes 0814D (WDB6703742N084257) T500 APS is a Plaxton Beaver 11 and was new in 1999.*

Above: *A 1997 14-seat Transit (BDVEVU36216), P249 VEH was purchased from Wigan Rental in November 1999.*

Above: *The last entry to the Johnson fleet in 1999 was P380 CBV, a 14-seat Transit with chassis number BDVEVM3468.*

The operators in the East Mainland were very few in number, as this part of Shetland has very few communities. In the north is Toft, the new crossing point for Yell Sound, which is a few miles north of Mossbank. This was the traditional crossing point for Yell, but change came about when the new pier was built at Toft in 1951, and the crossing over the sound to Ulsta was duly shortened. Further south come the villages of Vidlin and Nesting, both of which had bus operations based there.

A. P. SUTHERLAND

This was yet another one-bus operator, who was in business between 1948 and 1953. The firm of A. P. Sutherland was based at Vidlin on the east mainland. Sutherland, known to most of his passengers as Peter, operated a service twice weekly to Lerwick which ran on Mondays and Tuesdays. In order to expand his service he incorporated the nearby village of Nesting and started running to Lerwick four times a week using his Bedford WLB, with a 14-seat SMT body. The SMT body (seen above) was in fact a copy of the Duple body and built under license by SMT in Glasgow. The Bedford was purchased in 1948 at a time when commercial vehicles, especially PSVs, were in very short supply. It was already 14-years old by the time it came to Vidlin and naturally it did not last many more years. Sutherland's service continued down to 1953 at which time the vehicle was scrapped and Sutherland ended his operation.

W.C. HUNTER

W. C. Hunter of Nesting began business in 1948 at around the same time as Sutherland and he operated services into Lerwick with a 1937 Thornycroft. Few photographs have survived of this vehicle but it is seen in this line up third from the left. This is the only known surviving photographic evidence of this vehicle and the author would be delighted to find any further information on it; if such should be available! The Thornycroft was not a long lived vehicle and by 1952 it had been scrapped and replaced by a Bedford OWB. This was the second in a successive fleet of five coaches although Hunter was only ever a one-bus business. Each bus that Hunter purchased also had the distinction of ending its days with him whereafter the body would be scrapped or sold for a store or some other local enterprise.

Below: *This deplorable photograph is the only record of CSM 603, a Thornycroft Dainty bought from Alexander in 1948 by the operator W. C. Hunter of Nesting. It is seen in line-up at Lerwick in 1953 (third from the left), not long before it was scrapped in 1954.*

Above and Centre Right: *A. P. Sutherland's Bedford WLB (109342) with a SMT body, came from Georgeson & Moore, Scalloway in 1948 at 14-years of age. It is seen in the centre right picture with driver Willie Peterson. Five years later FS 8598 was scrapped in 1953.*

The Hunter fleet was as follows:

Reg.	Chassis	Body	Cap.	Year	Acq.
CSM 603	Thornycroft	?	C20F	1937	1948
ASD 100	Bedford OWB	Duple	B28F	1943	1954
SU 4099	Bedford OWB	Duple	B28F	1944	1957
FFS 885	Bedford OB	SMT	C25F	1948	1961
PS 1788	Austin K2SL	Fed. Ind.	B16F	1949	1968

Top Left: *Charlie Hunter's second bus ASD 100, was a Duple-bodied OWB obtained from his namesake, Hunter of Weisdale in 1954. No body or chassis numbers have been found for this vehicle, which was scrapped in 1957.*

Top Right: *Either SU 4099 or ASD 100 is seen hiding behind a pile of timber on the Victoria Pier at Lerwick. The ship behind is the Lerwick to Aberdeen ferry the* St. Clair.

Centre Right Top: *The firm's second OWB (11501) was this ex-Leask B28F SU 4099 seen here on the Nesting run. It was purchased in 1957 and scrapped four years later.*

Centre Right Bottom: *Another OB (76555) FFS 885 was Hunter's fourth bus; it had a SMT 25-seat body and was new to Highland Omnibus in 1948. The only picture we have of it shows it laying derelict behind his garage at Vassa, Nesting.*

Bottom: *The last vehicle in the fleet was this Federated Industries-bodied Austin K2SL (134985) registered PS 1788. It was purchased from Pat Isbister in Walls in 1968 and is seen at Lerwick whilst on service before it was scrapped in 1969.*

The Norse called the island of Whalsay 'Whale Island', but the 19th-Century name bestowed by Scottish fishermen, 'Bonnie Isle', seems more appropriate for an island that now has a population of around 1,000. It takes about 30 minutes to make a crossing by the modern ferry from Vidlin to Symbister, but public transport on the island has always been limited, despite the size of the fishing industry based here. Only two bus operators have been based in Whalsay, T.A. Arthur and the S.I.C.

T.A. Arthur

Thomas Arthur, known locally as Tammie, started out as a car hirer and did not get his first bus until 1965. This was a small 16-seat Karrier 20-cwt with a Reading body, which was acquired for school runs and private hire work. Over the years he had four public service vehicles, all of which were painted blue and cream. In 1977 the operation was taken over by the Shetland Islands Council (SIC), but Arthur's sole remaining vehicle (a Brush-bodied Bedford SB) was not considered to be of any use and it was duly scrapped.

Reg.	Chassis	Body	Cap.	Year	Acq.
20 NPP	Karrier	Reading	B16F	1960	1965
SL 3474	Bedford OB	Duple	C29F	1950	1968
PS 1991	Bedford OB	Mulliner	B28F	1950	1974
KGB 759	Bedford SB	Brush	C33F	1952	1976

Above: *Here we see SL 3474 and 20 NPP parked outside the Clydesdale Bank in Lerwick, this was also the stand for Georgeson & Moore and J. Johnson & Son who operated the Scalloway services.*

Centre Right: *Seen on Whalsay, 20 NPP was a 1-ton Karrier (D98A6554) with a Reading B16F body, which was purchased from Baldry of Bletchley in 1965 and scrapped in 1974.*

Bottom Right: *Purchased from John Leask & Son in 1968, SL 3474 was a Bedford OB (140027) with a 29-seat Duple Vista*

Top Left: *Obtained from H. Wood of North Roe, PS 1991 was a well-travelled Shetland bus by the time it reached its last operator in 1974. It is seen here awaiting arrival of the passenger ferry to Whalsay in the 1960s. It was scrapped on the island in 1976.*

Top Right: *Never a modern fleet, the last bus was KGB 759, the Brush-bodied Bedford SB. By the time it reached Whalsay from Unst it was 24-years old, and as the picture shows, more than a little dated. It was with this coach that he continued operations until 1979. The SB was later scrapped, but having lasted well into the era of preservation, it was a great pity that this rare survivor was not taken away for restoration.*

SHETLAND ISLANDS COUNCIL

In the scheme of things, it seems highly unusual for a municipal authority to be operating bus services today, especially following the de-regulation of buses during the Thatcher years. No longer do we see 'So and So' City Transport or 'Such and Such' Corporation on the side of buses and coaches, but in Shetland the SIC still runs a much-needed service. It began when T.A. Arthur decided that modernisation of his operation was not viable, and would probably have given up altogether had the SIC not stepped in. Arthur was retained as a driver/manager, but major maintenance work transferred to the council workshops in Lerwick. This public involvement in public transport was considered essential, in order to provide socially necessary services like school runs and a weekly shopper's service to Lerwick. However, following lack of support for the shopping service, this was abandoned and most of the work for the three buses is mainly schools and occasional private hire work.

Reg.	Chassis	Body	Cap.	Year	Acq.
TSU 633R	Bedford PJK	Plaxton	C29F	1977	1979
MSS 722P	Bedford J2SZ10	Caetano	C20F	1976	1979
XMS 295K	Bedford J2SZ10	Plaxton	B20F	1972	1980
KPS 600T	Bedford PJK	Plaxton	C29F	1978	1983
YCX 877V	Bedford PJK	Plaxton	C29F	1980	1984
E463 YDM	Mercedes 609D	PMT	C24F	1987	1989
F483 WFX	Mercedes 811D	Reeve Bur	C33F	1989	1993
J365 UNA	Mercedes 609D	Made to M	B24F	1992	1996
K546 OGA	Ford Transit	Deansgate	C15F	1993	1997

Centre Right Top: *The SIC's first Whalsay bus was Bedford PJK (FW455139) with a Plaxton Supreme body (77PJK007). Registered TSU 633R it came from Southern of Barrhead in 1979 and was scrapped in 1990.*

Centre Right Bottom: *This Caetano 20-seat body (75/15), was a Bedford J2SZ10 (DW111271) from 1976. Obtained from Law of Bucksburn in 1979, MSS 722P was scrapped in 1983.*

Bottom Right: *XMS 295K was yet another Bedford J2SZ10 (IT186325), but this time it had the dated Plaxton Embassy 20-seat body (728026). This 1972 coach came to Whalsay from Shalder in 1980 and was scrapped four years later.*

Top Left: *I know this vehicle quite intimately, as it was in our fleet from new in 1978, until it was sold to the SIC in 1983. Registered KPS 600T, it was a Bedford PJK (HW450007) with a Plaxton Supreme 29-seat body (728026). It is seen here on Victoria pier, Lerwick some time before it was sold in 1993. It was badly vandalised in 1995 and later scrapped.*

Top Right: *Next in the fleet was the Huddersfield registered YCX 877V dating from 1980, one of a succession of coaches to come from West Yorkshire to Shetland. This was yet another Bedford PJK (KW450230), with a Plaxton Supreme 29-seat body (80PJK006) which had been bought from Bethell of Reddish in May 1984. It lasted with the SIC until 1995,*

Centre Left Top: *Obtained from Green's of Kirkintulloch in March 1989, the SIC had E463 YDM in service on Whalsay until 1998, when it was exchanged for a Ford Transit mini-bus from J.F. Johnson & Son, Brae. This Mercedes 609D (668063-20-839194) had a 24-seat PMT body, and dated from 1987.*

Centre Left Bottom: *Another Mercedes to work on Whalsay, F483 WFX, had a 29-seat Reeve Burgess body. It was mounted on a 811D chassis (670303-20-938462) dating from 1989. It was acquired by the SIC from Timms & Presley of Bolton in January 1993 and it is still working on the island.*

Bottom Left: *Already discussed under the section dealing with J. F. Johnson & Son, Brae, we see the Ford Transit mini-bus K546 OGA. It was traded for the Mercedes 609D E463 YDM and is still at work with the SIC.*

Bottom Right: *The SIC's final acquisition (from Walsh of Middleton in 1996) was J365 UNA, a Mercedes 609D (6680632P163981) with a Made to Measure 29-seat body conversion. Prior to arriving on Whalsay it had also been registered as J9 JPT and J614 PNE. It is one of the three SIC coaches still working on the island at the time of writing.*

Facing out in to the Atlantic Ocean, the Western Mainland contains the communities of Sandsound, Reawick, Westerwick, Aith, Bixter, Gruting, Walls, Sandness and West Burrafirth, the latter of which is the terminal for the ferry service to Papa Stour. Another ferry service runs from Walls to the most westerly island of Foula, and takes around five hours.

PETER ISBISTER

This well-known operator from the village of Walls began his work in the Shetland bus industry with T.L. Sinclair of Lerwick. His main service was providing a stage carriage route between Lerwick and Walls, and it was on this route that Peter Isbister worked as a driver. When Sinclair retired from the business in 1955, he passed over the sole bus, a Bedford WHB with a Duple body, to Isbister. He kept this for a short while, but by this time it was quite elderly, and Peter then purchased his first 'new' vehicle, a second-hand 1939 Bedford M-Type. The business was continued successfully down to 1966, at which time it passed over to his son, Peter, who is still operating today.

Reg.	Chassis	Body	Cap.	Year	Acq.
FS 5896	Bedford WHB	Duple	B14F	1933	1955
WG 8487	Bedford WLG	Duple	C14F	1939	1955
PS 1788	Austin K2SL	Fed. Ind	C20F	1949	1963

Above: *A wonderful scene from Shetland life half a century ago, complete with period cars and buses is found in this view of the Reawick Regatta during the early-1950s.*

Centre Right Top: *One of the buses that I have not been able to find a picture for is FS 5896. This was a 1933 Bedford WHB (100103) with a 14-seat Duple body. It was acquired in 1955 from T. Sinclair of Lerwick, and looked similar to this official Bedford photograph shown here.* Vauxhall Motors

Centre Right Bottom: *Isbister's second Bedford, a WLG model (15845) with a Duple C14F body (6240). Registered WG 8478, it is shown here at Lerwick on service in approximately 1960. Bought from Johnson's of Scalloway in 1955, it went to Whalsay for use as a travelling shop in 1963.*

Bottom Right: *Also obtained from Johnson's of Scalloway was Austin K2SL (134985) with a Federated Industries C20F body, PS 1788 is seen here at Lerwick bus park in or around 1964.*

PAT ISBISTER

As stated previously Peter Isbister passed his business on to his son, also called Peter, but better known as Pat. As a result he took over his father's solitary vehicle (PS1788) in 1966, which he ran until 1968. At this time he obtained the OB seen above, and two years later he acquired a second vehicle - a Bedford SBG - in 1970. Since then he has usually operated two coaches, along with a mini bus and private hire cars as well.

Pat continued his father's service into Lerwick, but gave this up to Shalder Coaches in 1979. It was then operated by John White for a while, but recently went to Rapsons. Isbister's still provide a connecting mini-bus service from Sandness and Dale of Walls into Walls village. The bulk of their work today is school children and private hire. The company is still based in Walls, and not far from the sea shore near the end of the Voe. From time to time this has caused the occasional problem for Pat, as the Atlantic Ocean (no respecter of property) has built up against the shore and flooded into his garage.

At the time of writing, one of his former coaches, DRL 436V the Ford R1014 with a 33-seat Duple Dominant II body, has just passed into preservation. Although this event has taken place in the autumn of 2000 (and thus beyond the scope of this work), we make mention of it now, because the new owners of the coach are Trans-Pennine, the publishers of this book.

Reg.	Chassis	Body	Cap.	Year	Acq.
PS 1788	Austin K2SL	Fed. Ind.	C20F	1949	1966
SS 7237	Bedford OB	Duple	C29F	1949	1968
SGB 359	Bedford SBG	Duple	C41F	1956	1970
603CYS	Bedford C5C1	Duple	C29F	1961	1973
FWT 322C	Bedford SB5	Plaxton	C41F	1965	1975
PGM 638H	Bedford VAM	Duple	C45F	1970	1977
PSE 56M	Bedford VAS	Duple	C29F	1973	1981
YNF 350T	Bedford NJM	Duple	C41F	1978	1987
DRL 436V	Ford R1014	Duple	C33F	1980	1991
WFW529W	Bedford YLQ	Plaxton	C45F	1981	1994
N603 FWA	Ford Transit	Ford	C14F	1996	1999

Opposite Page Top: *As stated on page 45, the business of Peter Isbister was taken over by his son Pat in 1966, who inherited one single coach from his father. This was PS 1788 an Austin K2SL (134985) with a Federated Industries C20F body, which had later been reduced to just 16-seats. It dated from 1949 and was 17-years old by the time Pat got it in 1966. Two years later it was sold to W.C. Hunter of Nesting, when this Bedford OB (109966) with a Duple Vista body (54296) was purchased from J.A. Leslie of Virkie. SS 7237 is seen here in Lerwick with the firm's early colours of blue and grey and Pat Isbister at the wheel.*

Opposite Page Centre Left: *In 1970 a second vehicle, a Bedford SBG was purchased and with the start of a 'fleet' Pat changed his colours to red and cream. Here we see SS 7237 in its new livery, at Walls sometime during the early 1970s. The OB would in fact last until it reached 25-years old, and was finally withdrawn in 1974.*

Opposite Page Bottom Left: *As stated above, the Isbister colour changed to red and cream after the purchase of SGB 359 in 1970. This was yet another Bedford, but this time a SBG (50097) with a Duple Super Vega 41-seat body (1074/218). It dated from 1956 and was purchased in 1970 from Easton's of Inverurie. This coach lasted with Isbister until 1975, when it was sold to A.J. Eunson of Sumburgh.*

Top Right: *In February of 1973 the fleet increased to three vehicles, when a Bedford C5C1 (5068) was purchased from Riddler of Arbroath. This was 603 CYS, which had a 29-seat Duple Vista body (1140/1) that had been new to MacBrayne's in May 1961. This coach could be seen working around Walls until 1982, after which it came to us at Cullivoe for a short while before it was sold into preservation. It has since been restored in the MacBrayne livery of red, green and cream.*

Centre Right (top and bottom): *With the departure of SGB 359 in February 1975, a 10-year old Bedford SB5 (96233) was purchased from the operator Marshall of Baillieston. This had a MkI Plaxton Panorama body (652454) with 41-seats and was registered FWT 322C. It had been new to Hargreaves of Morley in 1965, along with a batch of three similar vehicles (EWT 277-9C) acquired by this firm in February-March 1965. At the end of the 1967 season it was traded in to the dealers, Hughes, who either sold it or loaned it to Baddeley Brothers of Holmfirth. It was repainted in their two-tone green livery and became fleet number 94. However, it did not remain long with this company and it was replaced by/swapped for sister coach EWT 279C in January 1968. It came to Shetland some seven years later wearing a blue and cream livery (picture centre right top), but the green was still visible beneath. After sometime in this livery, Pat Isbister repainted the coach into his red and cream livery (picture centre right bottom), which was retained until the SB was 'scrapped' in 1987. However, he did retain the name 'Princess Rose' that had appeared on the coach at some time during its history, and this lettering (along with vestiges of the Baddeley Brothers "Prince of Wales Plumes") can still be seen on the coach today. Thankfully, on disposal the coach was not actually scrapped, but turned into a hay shed on the moors above Walls. It still stands here at the time of writing, and is now the subject of a possible preservation attempt.*

Bottom Right: *New to the fleet of Central SMT (fleet no.C38) in 1970, was PGM 638H which is seen here in Lerwick in the late-1970s. It was one of the new generation Bedford VAM models (OT477531) and was fitted with a Duple Viceroy C45F body (211/30). It was purchased in June 1977 and lasted with Pat Isbister until 1980 when it went to Shalder Coaches of Scalloway, upon the arrival of DRL 436V a Ford R1014 with a Duple Dominant body.*

Left: *This was the seventh vehicle, bought by Pat Isbister, a Bedford VAS5 (CW456253) with a Duple Vista C29F body (263/1775). Registered PSE 56M, it was bought in April 1981 from Low of Tomintoul and sold to W. A. Rosie, Orkney, in 1990. Despite Pat's fondness for red and cream the livery never changed from green, and it can still be seen working in this guise on Orkney. The driver is my brother Victor Jamieson.*

Right: *Moving now to the eighth member of the fleet, we see YNF 350T at Mid-Yell school with children visiting from Aith school. The coach is yet another Bedford, this time a 1978 NJM (JW450265) with a Duple Dominant C41F body (914/1452). It was obtained from Franks of Haswell Plough in 1987 and lasted in service until 1994. It was sold to a dealer and the chassis was subsequently exported to South Africa.*

Left: *As my friends at Trans-Pennine Publishing will soon come to realise, washing down a coach is hard work! Here we see DRL 436V being washed at Walls, and the same sort of thing will occur now it has moved to my publishers at Appleby. It left Shetland on 27th October 2000, having arrived from Green's of Kirkintilloch in January 1991. This Ford R1104 (BDRCWJ37800) has a Duple Dominant II body (028/4906), and should provide 35 seats. However, the provision of an on-board WC has reduced the coach to C33F. The Ford has one other small claim to fame, in that it used to appear regularly in the Scottish Television 'soap' Take The High Road.*

Right: *The tenth vehicle in the fleet was a Bedford YLQ (KW450749) with a Plaxton Supreme II C45F body (8010QC025) which was registered WFW 529W. New in April 1981, it was purchased from Field of Newent in June 1994 and is still at work in the Walls area today. Following the departure of DRL 436V, it has since been joined by the ex-Watt's Ford D741 WRC which returned to Shetland just prior to the completion of this book. In this view Pat waves to the camera as he leaves Gutcher ferry terminal after returning from a trip to Unst.*

Left: *In addition to coaches, the Isbister family also operate hire cars and this Ford Transit mini-bus (BDVETG76742), with a 14-seat capacity, provides a natural link between the cars and the coaches. It was new in August 1996, and was obtained from T.L.S. of Salford in June 1999. As we go to press this vehicle is still working at Walls, doing a mixture of school runs and private hire jobs.*

JOHN ANDERSON

John Anderson was another one-bus operator, and he was based at Walls, from where he operated a converted ambulance as a 14-seat PSV on school services. This 'bus' is pictured above close to the attractive Burrastow House Hotel, a few miles beyond Walls and near the seaward end of the Voe. This popular tourist location has seen many visiting coaches over the years, but few as unusual as this Albion ambulance, which was purchased in 1949 and lasted until 1952. It is recorded that FMG 278 was so under-powered that, as it went up the hills around Walls, schoolboys on push-bikes would reach out and grab the rear handles on the vehicle and be pulled sedately up the inclines. It was scrapped in 1952, after Anderson gave up the business.

BERTIE JAMIESON

North of Walls lays the small village of Sandness and it was from here that Bertie Jamieson began his coach business in 1949. This was another post-war development in public transport in Shetland, albeit only a one-bus business commenced with a 1937 Bedford WTB. Few details of this vehicle have been preserved, and we only have poor photographs to illustrate it. In the centre picture the Bedford is second from the left, and from this we can determine that it carried a 25-seat Plaxton body. The Scarborough firm of F. W. Plaxton had begun an association with Bedford in late-1933, but the majority of Bedfords at this time were bodied by Duple, and the Bedford-Plaxton combination was not all that prolific. Therefore this was an unusual vehicle in Shetland, and as far as I can tell was the only one of its kind to operate here. Registered WF 9750, the Bedford was used on a service to Lerwick two days a week from 1949 onwards. The business continued until 1956, after which the Bedford was scrapped at almost 20-years of age.

Centre & Bottom Right: *Bertie Jaimeson's pre-war Bedford, WTB was some 12 years old by the time it arrived in Sandness and thereafter the Plaxton body sported a green and cream colour scheme. Jamieson only ever had the one vehicle and it lasted with him until 1956. Neither photograph is particularly clear but they again provide a valuable record. It is interesting that the lower photograph in the picture, showing the rear end of the coach at a local wedding, was actually taken on the occasion of Bertie's own marriage in 1953.*

G.W.N. WILLIAMSON

The firm of G.W.N. Williamson was another small business operated from the West Mainland and it began around 1948. At this time George Williamson purchased the little Chevrolet SB 3866 pictured on page 51 (although few details about its time with Williamson are known). It was followed in 1954 by the Bedford MLZ pictured above, which had the chassis number 28511 and a 19-seat SMT body. I thought that the colour scheme on AGS 677 may have been changed, but in fact it was was kept in Johnson's blue and cream. Williamson's work centred mainly around the transportation of school children.

Williamson also utilised his vehicles on Saturdays to do a run from Gruting into Lerwick via Bixter and Whiteness. The little Bedford that Williamson purchased from Johnson's of Scalloway continued on such services until 1964, however, by this time it was considerably time-expired and it was duly scrapped. An Austin LD (MSLD02A) with a 13-seat Kenex body was purchased as a replacement from Snape of Kennilworth. Finished in a red and cream livery, the registration number was 2810 AC, and it is pictured above. The business continued down until 1972 but at this time Williamson retired from the business and the LD was sold to J. W. Laurenson on Unst.

PETER SINCLAIR

A recent operator to start in the western mainland is Peter Sinclair of Skeld. This company began in 1994 when they started operating a 14-seat transit mini bus on school work. Since that time a further two vehicles have been added and the company and all remain in service today in the three-vehicle fleet.

Reg.	Chassis	Body	Cap.	Year	Acq.
F872 LNB	Ford Transit	Williams	C16F	1989	1994
D900 UNS	Bedford PJK	Wright	B31F	1986	1998
V47 DPS	Citroen Relay	Advance	C16F	1999	New

Centre Left: *Purchased from the firm of Thorpe from Gondall on Humberside, this Transit (BDVVKM15295) has a Williams 16-seat body conversion. It was acquired at the age of 5-years in 1994.*

Centre Right: *Sinclair's second vehicle (D900 UNS seen at the Clickimin Leisure Centre in Lerwick) was a Bedford PJK (GT105121) with a 31-seat Wright body. Made in 1986 it was bought from Baildon of Guisley, West Yorkshire in 1998.*

Bottom Right: *The third vehicle bought new was V47 DPS a Citroen Relay mini bus (VF7233J4215728400) with an Advance body conversion to provide 16-seats.*

JAMES WATT & SON

Based in the village of Reawick, where their garage is seen in the picture above in or around 1977, this company started in the bus business in 1946. Like many of the other operators in Shetland they had begun much earlier and had sprung from a car hire-taxi business. Many of these operators also had small capacity buses, but again as these do not come into the 13-seat and above capacity, they are not recorded in this particular work. Along with the staple private hire and school work Watts operated a service into Lerwick. A basic service was operated from Reawick into Lerwick every day with the exception of Wednesday. A further service was operated into Lerwick on a Sunday night as this enabled passengers to be able to stay overnight in readiness to start work or school on the Monday morning. Ordinarily the service bus, once into Lerwick, would stay there all day and return on an evening with passengers coming home from their work in the 'big city'. James Watt began with a 1930 14-seat Chevrolet, and for those readers who are not aware, I would explain that Chevrolet preceded the popular Bedford make. Chevrolet, like Bedford and Vauxhall, were in fact part of the American General Motors and, prior to the commencement of Bedford trucks in 1931, Chevrolet had been a popular British bus from 1919. However, with the arrival of Bedford, Chevrolet went into a demise.

Above: *The Watt fleet in 1977 at Reawick (James is on the left and his son John is on the right), the coaches are NPS 734M, LSM 44, OJH 128D, HGE 219, GUP 775H.*

Centre Right: *By the time the SC 7513 (chassis no. U65407) came to Reawick it was already 16-years old and for a lightly-built small-capacity bus it did not see many more years service, finally succumbing in 1949 when it was scrapped.*

Bottom Right: *The second bus, SB 3866, another Chevrolet (73268) from 1931, was purchased from Johnson of Scalloway in 1947. It was sold to G.W.N. Williamson of Grutting in 1948.*

The Watt fleet was:

Reg.	Chassis	Body	Cap.	Year	Acq.
SC 7513	Chevrolet	?	C14F	1930	1946
SB 3866	Chevrolet	?	C14F	1931	1947
PS 1805	Austin K2SL	Fed. Ind.	B20F	1949	New
PS 1999	Bedford OB	Mulliner	B28F	1950	New
SY 8878	Bedford OB	Duple	C29F	1948	1960
LSM 44	Bedford OB	Duple	C29F	1951	1964
HGE 219	Bedford OB	Duple	C29F	1950	1968
OJH 128D	Bedford VAS1	Duple	C29F	1966	1974
GUP 775H	Bedford SB5	Duple	C41F	1970	1977
KPS 701T	Bedford YLQ	Plaxton	C45F	1979	New
HUT 4V	Bedford YLQ	Plaxton	C45F	1980	1988
D471 WRC	Ford R1014	Plaxton	C45F	1987	1991
H854 AUS	Ford Transit	Deansgate	C14F	1991	New

Above: *In 1949 Watt took a big plunge for a small operator and purchased a brand new Austin K2SL (135527) with a 20-seat body by Federated Industries. This vehicle, PS 1805, remained with Watt's until 1968 when it was sold to the Sandwick Transport Company.*

Centre Left: *In 1950 a second new bus was purchased, this time PS 1999 a Bedford OB with a Mulliner body. Over the years that followed a number of Bedfords were purchased by the Watt family, as will be seen from the pictures that follow. This vehicle had the chassis number 141679, and the body number T563; it was eventually sold to our firm in 1960.*

Bottom Left: *Here we see SY 8878 on Watt's stand at the lower bus station in Lerwick. This OB (88725 had the 29-seat Duple Vista body (52217) and dated from 1948, and was purchased as a 12-year old coach from Johnson & Son, Scalloway in 1960. It was retained for eight years before being sold to J.G. Hunter on Unst in 1968.*

For many years the Bedford OB was a mainstay of Shetland bus operations, and even when this popular model was dying out in mainland Britain, it remained hard at work in the northern and western isles. As a result many bus enthusiasts came north to photograph and record these vehicles still at work in the late 1960s and early 1970s, and from various sources I was supplied with copies of their pictures. As few of the prints and slides that were sent to me carried any copyright information, or even the name of the donor, it has been difficult for me to give credit where it is due. I must therefore let the pictures in this book act as a record of this period, and by adding these pictures to the thousands I have taken over the years I have been able to compile this record. I can only say thank you to those who have helped, and hope that they will appreciate picture spreads like this one of the James Watt OBs at work in Shetland.

Top Right: *Here we see LSM 44 on the Watt's stand in Lerwick, it had chassis number 146795 and what we believe was Duple Vista body 54289. It was purchased from Johnson's of Scalloway in 1964 and finally scrapped in 1979. In the background can be seen another interesting array of vehicles, including the ubiquitous Volkswagen 'Beetle'.*

Centre Right: *The next OB purchased by James Watt was HGE 219 (chassis no. 137703) with Duple Vista C29F body (54759). It is seen leaving Lerwick opposite King Harold Street junction on the way north to Reawick with John Watt (the owner's son) at the wheel.*

Below: *Another view of HGE 219, this time seen parked at the Market Cross, Lerwick. The sign on the shop advertises 'K' Shoes. Bought in 1968 and sold to Kestrel Coaches in 1979, HGE is now in the 'Paradise Collection' belonging to the demolition contractor and haulier John Mould from Reading. It has since lost its registration plate to another Bedford, but it lives to fight another day.*

Left: *The eighth member of the James Watt & Son fleet was this Bedford VAS1 (6807116), dating from 1966. It had the new Duple Bella Vista C29F body (1201/18), which had a modified front end from the earlier models. Here we see OJH 128D , formerly with King Construction of Glasgow, with James Watt (the company founder) at the wheel. The livery has now changed from the earlier blue and cream to a sky blue and ivory scheme.*

Right: *In March 1977, Little's of Annan (Dumfriesshire) sold this Bedford SB5 (OT474830) to James Watt & Son. It had been new to General Motors of Chester-le-Street in 1970 and has the Sunderland registration GUP 775H. It carries the Duple Vega 31 body (216/3) which has dispensed with the raked rear window column on the earlier Bella Vista, Bella Vega and Vega Major models. It was supposedly scrapped in 1991, but has recently turned up (minus wheels), and is currently being considered for preservation by the Viking Coach Trust.*

Left: *Here we see HUT 4V and KPS 701T on Victoria pier, Lerwick awaiting tourists from a cruise liner, with John Watt standing between the two. Of these two coaches KPS 701T was a Bedford YLQ (JW451717) with a Plaxton Supreme IV C45F body (7910QX503). It was purchased new in January 1979 and sold to Leask's of Lerwick in 1991. The second 45-seat coach, HUT 4V was another Plaxton-bodied (7901QC051) Bedford YLQ (JW456931). This had been acquired from Green's of Kirkintilloch in November 1988, and was sold to Robinson & Morrison of Weisdale in 1996.*

Right: *John Watt remained with Bedfords until January 1991 when a new Ford Transit (BDVVLM09300) was purchased with a Deansgate 14-seat body. This signalled a change from the traditional blue and cream/blue and white livery and carried a white, yellow and blue colour scheme in a modern design. The Transit remained in the Watt fleet until the business ceased operation in 1996, at which time it went north to Unst, where it joined the fleet of P&T Coaches.*

Left: *Watt's final purchase was a Ford R1014 (D741 WRC), which came as a 4-year old vehicle in 1991. This was a fairly late offering from Ford, and was probably amongst the last batch of coach chassis built by them - it had the chassis number BCRSWP408170. Fitted with a Plaxton Paramount I C45F body (8710FTP2001, it was built in 1987. It was purchased from Slack of Tansley in August 1991 and was eventually sold to P & T Coaches on Unst in 1996. Watt's business sadly came to an end in 1996 when vital contracts were lost to a competitor. James Watt's son, John (who had run the business for several years), decided that private hire was insufficient to continue the business and the vehicles were sold. However, this popular character is still well known to many passengers in Shetland as he now drives for John Leask & Sons.*

L. GARRIOCK

In 1949 Laurence Garriock, better known locally as Lowrie, acquired the business of R. A. Johnson. He also obtained Johnson's only bus, a Bedford WLB with a canvas roof. This was used in the early years to provide the service run by Garriock from Wester Wick to Lerwick via Reawick, Sand, Bixter, and Whiteness, which ran on Tuesdays and Fridays. In the years that followed a Bedford OWB and a Bedford OB were bought along with a second OB obtained for spares not long before the business ceased to trade in 1967. The remaining vehicle SMY 140 was scrapped at the time the business came to its end.

Reg.	Chassis	Body	Cap.	Year	Acq.
VD 1065	Bedford WLB	Duple	C14F	1931	1949
WG 9816	Bedford OWB	SMT	B28F	1942	1951
SMY 140	Bedford OB	SMT	C25F	1947	1965
FFS 902*	Bedford OB	Duple	C29F	1947	1962

* Acquired for spares from Ganson Bros., Lerwick

Top Right: *This was VD 1065, a Bedford WLB (100003), the first vehicle in the business and the third-ever WLB to be made by Bedford. It was fitted with a 14-seat Duple body and was purchased from R. A. Johnson, Reawick in 1949. It lasted with Garriock until 1956, at which time it was scrapped and the body used for domestic purposes before being broken up some time afterwards.*

Centre Right: *Garriock's second vehicle, WG 9816, was a 1942 SMT-bodied Bedford OWB (9971), purchased from Alexander Western (W108) in 1951. It remained at work in Shetland for several years and was finally scrapped in 1965*

Below: *The third and last vehicle was SMY 140, which had an 'economy measures' SMT 25-seat coach body on a Bedford OB chassis (66968) - as can be seen by the absence of side flashes. The photograph was taken in Lerwick bus station, in or around 1960. Another OB (52510) was cannibalised in 1962 to provide spares for SMY 140.*

JOHN WHITE

Another newcomer on the Shetland bus scene is the firm of John White who are based at West Burrafirth, Bridge of Walls. White began his operations with a workman's service linking Mossbank and the oil terminal at Sullom voe. This service was sponsored by the Shetland Island Council and involved taking employees to work at Sullom and returning night shift workers back into Lerwick. This was a one way working and there was no corresponding trip on an evening. To work this service he purchased a Bedford YLQ with a 45-seat Plaxton Supreme body. His second purchase was a Ford Transit mini bus used on schools and private hire work. In the months and years that followed, White's fleet expanded mostly with new vehicles, his latest acquisitions both being Volvos.

Reg.	Chassis	Body	Cap.	Year	Acq.
DFS 570S	Bedford YLQ	Plaxton	C45F	1978	1994
D71 XPS	Ford Transit	Ford Conv	C14F	1986	1987
N162 KPS	Scania	Wright	B47F	1995	New
N416 KPS	Volvo B6-50	Wright	B38F	1995	New
N762 KPS	Mercedes 711D	Plaxton	B29F	1996	New
P442 LPS	Mercedes 711D	Plaxton	B29F	1996	New
N921 BWA	Mercedes 412	Autobus	B15F	1997	1998
T510 APS	Volvo B10MBLE	Alexander	B47F	1999	New
V258 DPS	Volvo B10MBLE	Wright	B47F	1999	New

Above: *A view of White's vehicles in service with V258 DPS and N162 KPS at the Viking Bus Station in Lerwick 1999.*

Centre Left: *The firm's first coach, was this Bedford YLQ (2DZ0GW454936), which had a Plaxton Supreme C45F body (7810QCM039) and was built in 1978. It was purchased from Macgillivary of Acharacle in 1994, and sold to ourselves for spares in 1999. It was registered DFS 570S.*

Bottom Left: *Next came D71 XPS, a 14-seat 1986 Ford Transit D71 XPS (BDVZGU33334), ex-Herrislea House Hotel. It lasted until 1999 when it was scrapped.*

Right: *Here we see N162 KPS the first new vehicle purchased by Whites Coaches. It is a Scania (L113CRL1824670) with the new Wright (Ultra-Low) body (U61-6.95). This 47-seater is to Diptac specification, with a very low floor-entry height and one of the first of this breed. John White (the owner) is pictured in the door. The bus arrived in Shetland in the summer of 1995, and is still working in the fleet today.*

Left: *Next to enter the fleet was N416 KPS, a Volvo B6-50 (YV3R36E17 SC005881) with a Wright Crusader B38F body (U36 6.95). It was purchased new in November 1995, and is seen here at the bus station in Lerwick. It lasted in the fleet until July 1999 when it was traded in against another Volvo T510 APS.*

Right: *Purchased new in December 1995, was N762 KPS a Mercedes 711D, with chassis number WDB6693032NO33475. It had a Plaxton Beaver B29F body (4938), and was again built to Diptac specification.*

Left: *Registered P442 LPS, this Mercedes 711D (WDB6693032NO44797) carries the Plaxton Beaver II body (6487), which has a seating capacity of 29. It has Diptac specification and is pictured here at the firm's garage with Scalloway on the destination blind.*

Right: *This Mercedes 412 Sprinter (WDB9044632P530093) was provided with an Autobus 'Classique' body conversion (1313). Registered N921 BWA, this was a former Mercedes demonstrator that was first registered in August 1997, and joined the White fleet in 1998. It is pictured outside our garage at Cullivoe, following a visit to Yell for a re-paint.*

Top Left: *Carrying a destination sign for Toft in the front window T510 APS awaits its next run. This Volvo B10MBLE (YV3R4A518 XA005360) has an Alexander LLX200 body (9910/8). It was purchased new in July 1997, and once again meets all the specifications for a modern service bus, as it gives low floor entry for the benefit of the elderly, disabled, and passengers with small children. This type of vehicle is a far cry from what was running north out of Lerwick a quarter of a century ago, and one wonders what the drivers of those days would think about the modern buses now in service.*

Centre Left: *Registered R460 VOP this vehicle, loaned to White in 1999, was a Volvo B10MBL (YV3RA4518TA002744). It had a Wright Renown (B44F) body (W353), and was new in 1997. It came to Shetland for a three month period during the summer of 1997, and afterwards was returned to Volvo at Warwick. This loan obviously influenced the company's future purchases.*

Below: *As readers will have noticed, there has been a considerable improvement in passenger facilities at Lerwick in recent years, and on 22nd May 1991 a new bus station was opened on the site of the town's lower bus station. Rejoicing in the name, Viking Bus Station, it provides a much smaller parking area than before, but this is adequate for today's traffic. The exit from the Viking Bus Station is shown to good effect in this picture of V258 DPS, the latest vehicle in the White fleet. It is another Volvo B10MBLE (YV3R4A517 XA005477), but it is fitted with a B47F Wright Renown body (B417). Purchased new in 1999, the vehicle is a current member of the White fleet and is photographed whilst departing on a service to Hillswick.*

ALAN LEASK

The next operator to be considered in Western Mainland was Alan Leask who was based in the village of Aith. He began his coach business in 1953 using the Bedford WTB with a C20F Duple body pictured left. With this elderly vehicle (it was already 16-years old when bought) Leask's service was run from Aith to Lerwick via Bixter. Unfortunately the operation was not sufficiently remunerative to remain viable and by 1956 it had gone out of business. The coach, despite being almost 20-years old, was still of some use and Leask sold WG 5772 to A. J. Eunson of Sumburgh in1956. The photograph on the left shows the 1937-built WTB (111074) with a ladies outing around 1954-1955.

R & M COACHES

One of the shortest lived ventures in the history of Shetland transport was the operation of R & M Coaches started by the Nicolson family in April 1987. They operated the Bedford YRT (EW456419) with a Caetano Moseley Continental 49 seat body (76-1) seen right. This coach was produced in 1976 and was purchased from Scott Rosehearty in April 1987. R & M Coaches advertised for private hire work but little appears to have been forthcoming perhaps with the exception of a few dance trips. With the venture being unsuccessful the Bedford remained parked in Bixter for a little while and was eventually scrapped about two years ago.

HERBERT NICOLSON

A more successful venture by the Nicolson family was that run by Herbert Nicholson of Bixter. He purchased a Ford Transit mini bus (BDVWHK69821) with a Mellor C16F body (52368), which is seen in the picture on the left. Dating from 1987 E974 MSE was obtained from Glennie of New Mill in October 1990. As will be noted from the school children sign in the front window the primary purpose of the Transit was school runs but a little private hire work was also undertaken. This business remained in operation until 1997 when the mini bus was sold to Shalder Coaches of Scalloway. At this time Herbert Nicolson retired from the business.

CREIGHTON WILLIAMSON.

Williamson had operated smaller mini buses for a number of years and purchased his first 13+ seat vehicle in 1996. It was very much a side line to his primary business, running the local store, and as a result was somewhat short lived. The bus side of the business ended in 1997 when the Mercedes N995 KUS (seen right) was sold to an operator in the Aberdeen area.

ROBINSON & MORRISON

Operating out of Weisdale, Robinson & Morrison started off doing school work. Four years ago they started a service from Whiteness and Weisdale into Lerwick mainly carrying OAPs, but it was also a full stage carriage service. This return working was only done one day every alternate week and this is still the current situation. Two years ago they started doing a one-way late night service from Lerwick to Walls.

Reg.	Chassis	Body	Cap.	Year	Acq.
B370 YHS	Ford Transit	Mellor	C16F	1984	1985
G767 CPS	Mercedes 811D	Reeve Bur	C25F	1990	New
L208 HPS	Ford Transit	Deansgate	C15F	1993	New
HUT 4V	Bedford YLQ	Plaxton	C45F	1980	1996

Top Left: *This Transit (BDVPDM28829) B370 YHS, came from Andenon of Beith in 1985 and was sold to Spiggie's in 1989.*

Centre Left: *Mercedes 811D (670303-20-972422) G767 CPS, has a Reeve Burgess C25F body and was bought new in 1990.*

Bottom Left: *Another new Transit (BDVLPR88410), L208 HPS, came new in August 1993 with a Deansgate C15f body.*

Bottom Right: *The most recent addition to the fleet was Bedford YLQ (JW456931) HUT 4V, purchased from J. Watt in 1996. It has a Plaxton C45F body and was new in 1980.*

C. H SMITH

The village of Whiteness was the base for C. H. Smith, better known as Charlie, who began business in 1953 with a 1944 Austin K2W. This vehicle had been purchased from Duncan's of Motherwell, it had just 14-seats and was used on a restricted service into Lerwick. We do not know of other types of work it may have undertaken but it probably would have done some private hire work and may also have been used like many other Shetland buses on the run to the Kirk on Sundays. We have no details as to why C. H. Smith finished his service, but it came to an abrupt end in 1958, after which the Austin was sold to Irvine Bros. of Boddam for spares.

Above: *Seen in Lerwick during the mid-1950s, is C. H. Smith's wartime Austin K2 (64868) GM 367 dating from 1944. It was this operator's only vehicle and we have no record of the body type, save that it carried 14-seats.*

HUNTER BROS

Another one-bus business was based in nearby Weisdale, this was commenced by the Hunter Bros. We have little detail about this operation other than it ran into Lerwick using a Bedford OWB purchased from W. Thomson of Sandwick. The service began shortly after the acquisition of the OWB in 1950 and came to an end in 1954, again we have few details regarding the demise of this service and it does not appear as though it was taken over by any other operator.

Bottom Right: *Based in Weisdale the Hunter Brothers had just one vehicle, ASD 100 a Bedford OWB with a Duple Utility body that dated from 1944. It is seen here having a tight squeeze through the narrow Commercial Street in Lerwick sometime during the early 1950s.*

ANDREW MORRISON

Based in the village of Whiteness, Andrew Morrison started off doing school runs from the village (and surrounding area) to the High School at Lerwick and this was supplemented by an amount of private hire work. This was all he did until 1977 when he joined Shalder coaches, becoming a part-owner of the Scalloway-based company. In 1997 he acquired a brand new Marshall 27-seater for carrying disabled elderly passengers. This work was carried out for about two years until Rapsons took over the Shalder fleet, and they made him give up his operators licence as a condition of the sale. Although he was a shareholder of Shalders, he did the disabled bus service in his own account.

Reg.	Chassis	Body	Cap.	Year	Acq.
456 DTR	Bedford SB 5	Duple	C41F	1963	1973
VNE 575	Bedford SB 3	Duple	C41F	1958	1974
P10 ASM	Marshall	SLF	C27F	1997	New

Top Left: *Purchased from Tricentrol in 1973, this Bedford SB5 (91762) was 10-years old when it arrived in Whiteness. It had an early Duple Bella Vega C41F body (1159/324), which featured the 'forced air' ventilation system that was fed from a roof-mounted 'scoop'. Registered 346 DTR the Bedford is seen at Lerwick's upper bus station in 1973.*

Centre Left Top: *After a while the blue and cream livery of 346 DTR was repainted to red with a black roof and the coach is seen in the new livery in 1974 outside Westings Hotel. This coach passed to Shalder in 1977. They eventually scrapped it, but the body still remains in a field on the West Mainland where it is used as a hay store.*

Centre Left Bottom: *Andrew Morrison acquired his second coach in 1974, when he purchased VNE 575 from Georgeson & Moore of Scalloway. This was a Bedford SB3 (59800) with a C41F Duple Super Vega body (1090/164). It lasted until 1976 when it was scrapped.*

Bottom Left: *In 1997 Morrison began operating this Marshall SLF (SMVFBL1R KTC105/089) with a 27-seat body. This did runs around Lerwick town centre picking up elderly and disabled passengers. Although a part-owner of Shalder Coaches, this vehicle belonged solely to Andrew Morrison and had the personalised registration plate P10 ASM.*

Opposite Page Top: *The Johnson Brothers fleet lined up at Scalloway sometime in the late 1950s. From left to right we see HGE 219, LSM 44, SY 8878 and PS 1788. The first three are all Duple-bodied OBs, the fourth coach is an Austin*

Opposite Page Centre Right: *This is the first bus owned by Johnson's with 13+ seats, RP 7689 was a Ford. Seen here in Main Street, Scalloway, this wonderful scene captures the atmosphere of the 1930s, but it has probably been a very long time since just three vehicles would have been parked in this street.*

Opposite Page Bottom Right: *Here we show a second picture of RP 7689, this time in closer detail. The vehicle dated from 1929, but there is no record of when it arrived in Scalloway, or where it came from; the record about its demise is also unclear.*

JAMES JOHNSON & SON

The first main operator to be based in Scalloway was the firm of James Johnson & Son, who began operating with horse-drawn lorries. Quite when passenger carrying began is not certain, but it seems as though some sort of hiring service was in place around the time of World War I. In 1921 a daily service was commenced with a 'motor bus' between Scalloway and Lerwick. For a short while this service was run alongside Alexander Cromarty (also of Scalloway), but details of this operation are sketchy. It is known that three locally-bodied Model T Fords were owned during this period, including PS 388, PS 398, and SA 5306. Seating capacity on these vehicles was very small.

As will be seen from the above picture, this firm employed a smart blue and cream livery which may have been applied to their first vehicle obtained in 1937. This was a Ford with an unknown body providing 14-seats. It was soon supplemented by a 1931 Chevrolet, probably one of the last built before Vauxhall began producing Bedford trucks and buses in 1931. Over the years the Johnson fleet grew, purchasing mostly second hand vehicles of the Bedford Marque. The pictures that follow on the next page show the progression of Bedford models over the years, ranging through the W and M types to the O and S. The last vehicle to be purchased was PS 2627, a Bedford SB with a Duple Super Vega body that had been brought new to the islands by John Leask in 1956. For a while Johnson's also operated KWX 412 the former Bedford/Vauxhall demonstrator that had been built in 1950 but not registered until 1951.

In 1968 the coach side of Johnson's was sold to John Leask & Son's of Lerwick, along with some of the buses, but the haulage side continued until 1970 when it was purchased by a friend of the Johnson family, Larry Sutherland. Starting with seven trucks, all Bedfords (of the O- S- and TK- type), Larry developed this side before changing the name to Sutherland Transport in 1973. In 1982 he acquired the Vauxhall dealership in Lerwick, and the Volkswagen dealership in Scalloway. The transport business was finally bought out by P&O Scottish Ferries in 1988. The car dealerships were retained until the summer of 2000 when Larry finally decided to retire.

To the majority of public service vehicle enthusiasts, any of the pictures in this book might be considered to be a 'Shetland Bus', but to Shetlanders this term has a completely different meaning. Here in Scalloway, between 1942 and 1945, a 'secret' base was used by Norwegian patriots who crossed the North Sea in fishing boats to bring back refugees from Norway in the one direction, and take spies, saboteurs and supplies for the resistance fighters in the other. Many of these boats were lost due to storms or enemy action, so the submarine-chasers *Hessa, Hitra* and *Vigra* were provided by the Royal Navy. This 'service' became known as **'The Shetland Bus'**, and an excellent book on the subject is published locally by *The Shetland Times*.

Reg.	Chassis	Body	Cap.	Year	Acq
RP 7689	Ford AA	?	C14F	1929	?
SB 3866	Chevrolet LQ	?	C14F	1931	?
WG 8478	Bedford WLG	Duple	C14F	1939	1944
PS 1788	Austin K2/SL	Fed. Ind.	C20F	1949	New
AGS 677	Bedford MLZ	SMT	C19F	1944	1950
CAV 269	Bedford OWB	SMT	B28F	1944	1951
HGE 219	Bedford OB	Duple	C29F	1950	1954
SY 8878	Bedford OB	Duple	C29F	1948	1954
LSM 44	Bedford OB	Duple	C29F	1951	1956
MPT 410	Bedford OB	Duple	C29F	1951	1958
KWX 412	Bedford SB	Duple	C33F	1951	1959
SL 3474	Bedford OB	Duple	C29F	1950	1963
VNE 575	Bedford SBG	Duple	C41F	1958	1966
PS 2627	Bedford SBG	Duple	C41F	1956	1964

Top Left: *An early view of SB 3866, Johnson's Chevrolet 73268), with an unknown 14-seat coach body. It is pictured climbing up Skord Hill. Scalloway castle in the background was built by the tyrant Earl Patrick Stewart using forced labour*

Centre Left: *This Bedford WLG (15845) with Duple body (6240) was bought from Alexander (No. W74) in October 1944, and it still retains the 'Bluebird' livery in this picture.*

Below: *Bought new in June 1949, PS 1788 was an Austin K2SL (134985) with a Federated Industries body. It is seen here in Castle Street, Scalloway.*

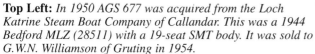

Top Left: *In 1950 AGS 677 was acquired from the Loch Katrine Steam Boat Company of Callandar. This was a 1944 Bedford MLZ (28511) with a 19-seat SMT body. It was sold to G.W.N. Williamson of Gruting in 1954.*

Top Right: *Next in the Johnson fleet came CAV 269 a Bedford OWB (18067) with a SMT body. Dating from 1944, it was acquired as a 7-year old vehicle from Leask's in 1951 and lasted until 1954 when it was sold to J. G. Hunter on Unst. Just the one picture has survived, and although it does not show the bus too clearly, it is a nice photograph of two herring gutters (Ruby Henderson and Martha Scollay) I think.*

Centre Right Top: *Already discussed under the fleet of James Watt & Son, this Bedford OB (137703) HGE 219 is seen in glorious colour on Victoria pier, Lerwick with the St. Clair in the background. The coach was purchased as a 4-year old vehicle from W. Thomson of Sandwick in 1954 and sold to James Watt in May 1968 just before Johnson's coach business came to an end.*

Centre Right Bottom: *A second OB (88725) to be sold to James Watt by Johnson's was SY 8878, which had a Duple Vista 29-seat body (52217). Seen here in Lerwick, it dated from 1948 and came from Todd, Mid Calder in 1954, before going to the Reawick operator in 1960.*

Bottom Left: *A third of Johnson's OBs would go to Watt in November 1964, this time LSM 44. This OB (146759) with Duple Vista body (54289), had come to Scalloway from Thomson of Sandwick in 1956.*

Bottom Right: *Another Duple-bodied (56618) OB (146361 in the Johnson fleet was MPT 410 from 1951, which came from the Sunderland operator (Heaviside) in 1958. It is seen entering Lerwick pier, followed by KWX 412 the Bedford SB that appeared at the Commercial Motor Show in 1950 and spent its formative years as a Vauxhall demonstrator.*

Top Left: *This Bedford SB had modified chassis and body numbers (3743/56794), which were allocated by Bedford in August 1951 when the coach was registered KWX 412 in the West Riding of Yorkshire. However it was put on the road in October 1950 with the chassis no SBL2 and no body number, as it was a Vauxhall-Bedford demonstrator. In 1951 it was completely refurbished and sold to an operator called Kildare near Doncaster. It then moved to a firm called Heap's of Leeds who used it on regular runs to Scarborough. At some stage during this ownership the original Duple service bus seats were replaced by a set of Plaxton coach seats, presumably this work was done during one of the vehicles runs to Scarborough. It was sold by Heap's to John Leask & Son in 1954 and then sold to Johnson's in 1959. It remained in their fleet until sold back to Leask's with the business in 1968. It was never again used by the Lerwick operator, and subsequently sold to work on the island of Yell.*

Centre Left Top: *The next purchase by the Scalloway operator was yet another OB (140027) with a Duple Vista 29-seat body (56081). Dating from 1950 SL 3474 came from John Leask & Son in March 1963, and lasted until it was sold to T.A. Arthur on Whalsay in June 1968. It is seen here at the Scalloway bus stand in Lerwick, alongside Georgeson & Moore's Austin.*

Centre Left Bottom: *Here we show PS 2627, a Bedford SBG (44895), with a 7ft 6in wide Duple Super Vega 41-seat body (1060/388). This was the last coach to be purchased by the Johnson brothers, one of whom (Hindie Johnson) is wearing the cap. The gentleman on the right is a courier for Midland Red, a coach operator who ran regular summer tours to Shetland but left their buses in Aberdeen and contracted local firms to operate tour services in the islands.*

Below: *This was actually Johnson's second last vehicle, but as it is pictured in full colour, we have taken the opportunity to present it in a large format. This is VNE 575 another Bedford SBG (59800) with a Duple Super Vega C41F body (1090/164). Both VNE 575 and PS 2627 were purchased from John Leask & Son, and they dated from 1958 and 1956 respectively. The purchase dates were 1966 and 1964, and both were still in the fleet when the business came to its end in 1968. At this time VNE 575 was sold to Georgeson & Moore, but PS 2627 went back to John Leask & Son. Both these pictures are taken at the bus stand by the Hygienic Store in Scalloway.*

GEORGESON & MOORE

Following World War II, Mitchell Georgeson and Bob Moore began to develop the Scalloway-Lerwick service, after they acquired the business of Alexander Cromarty on 1st October 1945. Cromarty previously had nothing larger than a 12-seater, but the two partners increased this capacity when they bought a pair of Bedford WLBs in 1945, followed by a Citroen in 1946 and another WLB in 1947. In 1950 the business, with two buses (EK 9251 and GTV 597) were sold to Lollie Young and Donnie Jamieson. They retained the name Georgeson & Moore, but began to expand the operation from Scalloway until selling out to the new Shalder Coaches company in 1977.

Reg.	Chassis	Body	Cap.	Year	Acq
FS 8598	Bedford WLB	SMT	C14F	1934	1945
VD 1065	Bedford WLB	Duple	C14F	1931	1945
FG 7210	Citroen		C20F	1931	1946
EK 9251	Bedford WLB	Duple	C20F	?	1947
AGS 675	Bedford ML2	SMT	C19F	1944	1950
GTV 597	Bedford OWB	Duple	B28F	1944	1950
NTU 269	Guy Vixen	?	C31F	1957	1952
PS 1407	Bedford OB	SMT	C29F	1946	1953
PS 1927	Austin CXB	Kenex	C32C	1950	1958
LTC 875	Austin CXB	Samuelsbury	C29F	1950	1959
SY 9964	Bedford SB	Duple	C37F	1951	1966
DYJ 833	Bedford SBG	Duple	C37F	1955	1964
VNE 575	Bedford SBG	Duple	C41F	1958	1968
PS 2627	Bedford SBG	Duple	C41F	1956	1972
272 MTM	Ford 570E	Duple	C41F	1964	1973
7284 LG	Ford 570E	Plaxton	C41F	1963	1973
GPS 730P	Bedford YRT	Duple	C53F	1975	New

Above: *Typical of Georgeson operations, PS 2627 and DYJ 883 are seen outside Lerwick's Thule Bar in the 1970s.*

Centre Right Top: *Bought in 1945, FS 8598 was a Bedford WLB (109342) from Shari of Manchester. Seen in Scalloway, the SMT-bodied coach was sold to A.P Sutherland in 1948.*

Centre Right Bottom: *The next WLB (100003) was VD 1065, which had a Duple body and was sold to R.A. Johnson of Reawick in 1947. It is seen on the right of the picture, whilst the rear of the Citroen FG 7201 is seen on the left.*

Bottom Right: *Few details have emerged on FG 7201, a 1931 Citroen with chassis number K1964 and an unknown C20F body. It was purchased from Johnson's of St. Andrews in 1946, and was scrapped in 1949 some months before the business was sold to Lollie Young.*

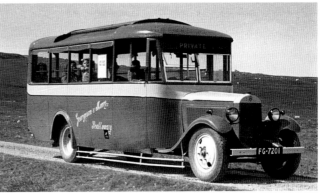

Left: *The next bus to enter the Georgeson & Moore fleet was EK 9251, a Bedford WLB with a C20F Duple body. We have few details about this vehicle, other than it came from Cheyne of Aberdeen and was scrapped in1950. This photograph of a similar vehicle in service with SMT (Scottish Motor Traction) is therefore a representative image.*

Right: *In 1950, around the same time that Johnson's of Scalloway bought AGS 677 from the Loch Katrine Steam Boat Company of Callandar, Georgeson & Moore bought an identical coach AGS 675 from the same firm. This was also a 1944 Bedford MLZ (28509) with a 19-seat SMT body. The vehicle was sold to the Irvine Brothers of Boddam at an unrecorded date for spares.*

Left: *GTV 597 was a Bedford OWB (143402) with a Duple 28-seat Utility body which came from Shipside of Nottingham. We have no other details about this acquisition, except that it was sold to Manson Brothers of Brae for spare parts. The OWB was a very utilitarian product, and was noted for the wooden slatted seats that gave a very uncomfortable ride. As soon as the English and mainland Scottish operators could get better replacements at the end of World War II, the OWBs were often sold to poorer firms.*

Right: *What has to have been one of the ugliest buses on Shetland was this Guy Vixen. Registered NTU 269 it has an unrecorded C31F body and arrived with Georgeson & Moore in 1952. I have a disposal date of 1957 for this coach after which I suppose it was scrapped; heaven forbid that it is still lurking around somewhere*

Left: *The eighth large bus in the Georgeson & Moore fleet was PS 1407, a Bedford OB (15088) with a SMT C29F body. It was new to W. Thomson of Sandwick in April 1946, and was sold to the Scalloway firm in April 1953; it was with Georgeson & Moore for eight years until 1961 when it went to the Manson Brothers of Brae. It is seen here at the north end of Commercial Street, in Lerwick, where the firm used to park.*

Above: *Next to join the fleet was PS 1927 an Austin CXB (143402) which had a Kenex C32 centre entrance body. It was sold to the firm by John Leask & Son in 1958, but this photograph was taken during the time it was still owned by the Lerwick firm. The driver is Sandy Laurenson, who was captured on film at Mavis Grind. The coach was scrapped in 1964.*

Right: *The next acquisition was another Austin CXB, and from the chassis number of 143408 it will be seen that both these vehicles must have been in the Midlands factory at the same time. Although just six serial numbers apart LTC 875 had the little-known 29-seat Samuelsbury body. The coach came from Grant of Bo'ness in 1959 and was scrapped in 1966.*

Left: *Shown in glorious colour, which reveals the black, cream and red livery, we see SY 9964 outside the Clydesdale Bank in Lerwick. This was a 1951 Bedford SB (1207) with a Duple Vega C33F body (56963) that was acquired from Leask's of Lerwick in 1966. After seven years service with Georgeson & Moore it was sold for use as a shed at Cott, where it was broken up in 1998. However, the windows survived as spares for KWX 412.*

Right: *Another lovely colour picture shows DYJ 833 at the Anderson High School in Lerwick, waiting to depart with a full load of passengers. This Bedford SBG (35441) had the Duple Super Vega body (1055/215), with what was known as the 'Butterfly Grill'. This stylish coach dated from 1955, and was purchased from John Leask in 1964. It was with Georgeson & Moore for 10-years, before being sold for use as a shed in 1974.*

Left: *The next two coaches in the Georgeson & Moore fleet were all Bedford SBGs with Duple Super Vega bodies, and each one had been in the fleet of John Leask. In 1968 they got VNE 575, chassis number 59800 with the later style of Super Vega C41F body (1090/164) from Johnson of Scalloway. Note the different style of side flash, which was a simplification of the earlier design. This coach dated from 1958 and was acquired in 1968 - it was sold to Andrew Morrison for schools work in 1974, when it was painted into a red and black livery. It is pictured here at the Scalloway bus stand in the early 1970s.*

Right: *PS 2627 was once the pride and joy of the Leask fleet, but it was sold to Johnson of Scalloway and re-purchased in 1968. It was then sold to Georgeson & Moore in 1972 and was transferred to Shalder Coaches in 1977. It still remains in Shetland today, albeit in a terribly derelict condition and is yet another SBG (44895). It had the 7ft 6in wide Super Vega body (1060/388) which was built by Duple in 1956. Waiting to depart Lerwick for Scalloway, this picture dates from the mid-1970s.*

Left: *This was not a common vehicle in Scotland, nor indeed were there many of these Ford 570Es (L80C854832) with the Duple Trooper C41F body (1173/53). In many ways similar to the Bella Vega body applied to the Bedford chassis of the mid-1960s, this coach dated from 1964. It was acquired from Miller of Flitwick in 1973, and passed to Shalder Coaches with the business in 1977. It is seen here passing Scalloway Hall with its driver, Alan Young.*

Right: *Another Ford 570E (L80B830759) to survive into the 21st-Century (as a derelict hulk) is seen here in happier days. This example has a Plaxton Consort IV C41F body (632694) and was registered 7284 LG. It was built in 1963 and came to Georgeson & Moore as a 10-year old vehicle from Auchenblae Motors in 1973. It was still working when the business was acquired by Shalder Coaches in 1977 and stayed in that fleet until 1980 when it was scrapped. In recent years it has served in a domestic role, part summer house, part store, but despite its very poor condition today, it still could be a candidate for preservation in the future!*

Left: *After years of buying second-hand vehicles, November 1975 saw the arrival of Georgeson & Moore's only new coach. This was GPS 730P a Bedford YRT (EW455326) with a Duple Dominant Express body (518/2625). However, not only was this the firm's first new vehicle but it was also their last. As stated, this company had been acquired from Mitchell Georgeson by Lollie Young in the 1950s, and by the mid-1970s it was being run by Lollie's sons Bobby and Alan. In 1977 Bobby wanted to move on and they sold the business to a new company, Shalder Coaches, although Alan would continue his coaching interests as a partner in the new venture!*

SHALDER COACHES

As noted before, Shalder coaches was formed in 1977 with three partners, these being Alan Young (son of the owner of Georgeson & Moore), Andrew Morrison (who we have already discussed on page 62) and Wilbert Sharp. The latter was the local Volvo car dealer, which perhaps explains why the firm later developed a fondness for Volvo coach chassis, At the start they continued to run the firm under the Georgeson & Moore name, but after a couple of years they began to take delivery of a new batch of vehicles. At this time they changed the livery from black and cream to black and white. As this was the colour of the plumage on the oyster catcher bird, known locally as the shalder, this name was duly adopted. The vehicles transferred from Georgeson & Moore to Shalder were as follows

Reg.	Chassis	Body	Cap.	Year	Acq.
PS 2627	Bedford SBG	Duple	C41F	1956	1977
7284 LG	Ford 570E	Plaxton	C41F	1963	1977
272 MTM	Ford 570E	Duple	C41F	1964	1977
GPS 730P	Bedford YRT	Duple	C53F	1975	1977

Above: *A line-up of Shalder vehicles at the Scalloway garage, inset the oyster catcher or shalder which figured largely in the company's logo.*

Centre Right: *Bedford SBG, PS2627, in the black and cream livery which was continued by the new operation for about two or three years after its formation. This Bedford remained at work with the company until 1980 when it was finally scrapped, yet this 24-year old coach was not broken up, although most of its 41-seats were taken out to make a greenhouse. It still remains at the time of writing, and is the subject of a potential preservation scheme.*

Bottom Right: *Another former Georgeson & Moore coach that was sold with the business, Ford/Plaxton 7284 LG was also sold for scrap in 1980 - yet 20-years on, it too has survived being broken up, and still remains as a depreciating hulk.*

Top Left: *Here we see one of the 'absorbed coaches 272 MTM parked outside Leask's garage. This Duple-bodied Ford would have made an interesting candidate for preservation, but I have no details regarding its disposal and must assume it was scrapped when the firm began to modernise their fleet.*

Centre Left: *With a similarly styled Duple body, we show 346 DTR, which was brought into the company by one of the new partners Andrew Morrison. Only very slight outward differences will be noted on this 1963 Bella Vega, from the 1964 Trooper shown above. This coach was scrapped in 1980, but 20 years later it is still surviving (but only just) as a hay store in the West Mainland.*

Below: *The early-1970s saw a fairly generous grant regime for coach operators wanting to upgrade their fleet, and many took the opportunity to purchase the new Duple Dominant body. The conditional 'express' two leaf doors were mandatory, as seen to good effect in this view of GPS 730P. This YRT (EW455326) with its C53F body (518/2625) lasted until 1999 when it went to the fire station at Sumburgh, where it was later scrapped.*

Vehicles Subsequently Acquired by Shalder Coaches

Reg.	Chassis	Body	Cap.	Year	Acq.
346DTR	Bedford SB 5	Duple	C41F	1963	1977
PGM 641H	Bedford VAM70	Duple	C45F	1970	1977
JSY 913H	Bedford VAS 5	Plaxton	C29F	1970	1977
SAY 810G	Bedford VAM70	Duple	C45F	1969	1978
KSY 365H	Bedford VAM70	Duple	C45F	1970	1978
WGM 43K	Bedford YRQ	Duple	C45F	1972	1978
HGM 339E	Bristol Lodekka	E.C.W.	H78F	1967	1979
WGM 44K	Bedford YRQ	Duple	C45F	1972	1979
XMS 295K	Bedford J2SZ10	Plaxton	B20F	1972	1979
399 ETB	Bedford SBG	Duple	C41F	1958	1980
LPS 850V	Volvo B58-56	Plaxton	C53F	1979	1980
MPS 666V	Volvo B58-56	Plaxton	C53F	1980	1980
MPS 970W	Volvo B58-56	Duple	C53F	1980	1980
GUP 860C	Bedford VAS 1	Duple	C29F	1965	1980

Reg.	Chassis	Body	Cap.	Year	Acq.
OPS 899X	Volvo B58-56	Duple	C53F	1982	1982
PPW 847M	Bedford YRT	Duple	C53F	1974	1982
PGM 638H	Bedford VAM 70	Duple	C45F	1970	1982
HWU 58N	Leyland	Plaxton	C53F	1975	1983
HWU 64N	Leyland	Plaxton	C53F	1975	1983
HWU 71N	Leyland	Plaxton	C53F	1975	1983
WRN 802V	Ford Transit	Dormobile	B16F	1980	1984
WDU 693S	Volvo B58-56	Caetano	C53F	1977	1984
OWT 1M	Volvo B58-56	Duple	C53F	1974	1984
NLS 256P	Bedford SB5	Duple	C41F	1976	1987
FSU 330	Volvo B58-61	Irizar	C45F	1981	1987
OPS 899X	Volvo B58-56	Duple	C53F	1982	1987
RNP 957P	Volvo B58-56	Plaxton	C53F	1976	1987
D660 XPS	Volvo B10M-61	Duple	C53F	1987	New
HNT 945N	Bedford PJK	Duple	C29F	1975	1987
MGG 396P	Bedford YRQ	Duple	C45F	1976	1987
PDO 639M	Volvo B58-56	Duple	C53E	1974	1988
719 CEL	Volvo B58-56	Plaxton	C53F	1973	1987
64 XYD	Volvo B58-56	Plaxton	C53F	1973	1987
PDO 639M	Volvo B58-56	Duple	C53F	1974	1988
D31 XSS	MCW MF150/10	MCW	C25F	1987	1988
HAY 777L	Bedford YRQ	Duple	C45F	1973	1988
LPS 210T	Bedford YLQ	Duple	C45F	1979	1988
VBM718W	DAF MB200	Plaxton	C57F	1981	1988
A416 SPS	Bedford YNT	Plaxton	C53F	1984	1988
A106 MAC	Bedford YNT	Plaxton	C53F	1984	1988
XWK 17X	Bedford YNT	Plaxton	C53F	1982	1988
NPS 256W	Bedford YLQ	Duple	C39F	1981	1988
A343 SPS	Iveco-Fiat	Caetano	C18F	1983	1988
LPS 963V	Bedford YLQ	Duple	C45F	1979	1988
OPS 465X	Ford Transit	Dormobile	C16F	1982	1988
HOR 322L	Bedford YRQ	Plaxton	C45F	1972	1988
USE 500R	Bedford YMT	Duple	C53F	1977	1988
F828 APS	Volvo B10M/60	Plaxton	C53F	1989	1989
F469 WFX	Volvo B10M/60	Plaxton	C57F	1988	1989
E593 UHS	Volvo B10M/46	Plaxton	C38F	1988	1989
E566 MAC	Talbot	Pullman	B22F	1988	1989
E568 MAC	Talbot	Pullman	B22F	1988	1989
PPP 139R	Bedford YLQ	Duple	C45F	1976	1990
E630 MAC	Talbot	Pullman	B22F	1988	1990
F938 TVC	Talbot	Pullman	B22F	1989	1990
H410 DPS	Volvo B10M/60	Plaxton	C57F	1990	1990
J75 FPS	Volvo B10M/60	Plaxton	C57F	1991	1991
G192 SCH	MCW MF154/2	MCW	C28F	1990	1993
D181 TSB	Volvo B10M/61	Plaxton	C57F	1986	1993
E609 YPS	Mercedes 811D	Reeve Bur	C29F	1988	1993
KPS 701T	Bedford YLQ	Plaxton	C45F	1979	1993
D982 NJS	Mercedes 609D	Dixon	C27F	1987	1994
FUJ 905V	Bedford YMT	Duple	C53F	1980	1994
E974 MSE	Ford Transit	Mellor	C16F	1987	1997
GBS 714P	Bedford YRQ	Duple	C45F	1976	1997
G639 BHP	Talbot	Pullman	B20F	1989	1997
C771 FBH	BedFord YNV	Duple	C53F	1985	1997
S388 JPS	MAN 11.22	Marshall	B36F	1998	1998
S389 JPS	MAN 11.22	Marshall	B36F	1998	1998

Top Right: *This 1970 Bedford VAM 70 (OT478366) with a 45-seat Duple Viceroy body (211/33) came from Central SMT (C41) in 1977. PGM 641H was sold to Johnson Bros. of Brae in 1981.*

Centre Right Top: *The next Bedford was a VAS5 (9T471778) registered JSY 913H with a Plaxton C29F (708071) which came from Stewart of Dalkeith in 1977. It is shown here at the pierhead in Lerwick sometime before it was scrapped in 1984.*

Centre Right Bottom: *SAY 810G was another Bedford VAM 70 (OT465639) with a Duple Viceroy C45F body (1226/206) dating from 1969. It was obtained from Turners of Ulleskelf in 1978 and was sold back to mainland Britain the year after.*

Bottom Right: *A further VAM 70 (OT478352), KSY 365H (also from 1970), joined the fleet from Glass of Haddington in 1978. It too had a Duple Viceroy C45F body (211/81), which lasted with Shalder until being sold back to mainland Britain in 1980.*

Above (both): *This is an early Bedford YRQ (2T472449), a chassis more commonly associated with the Duple Dominant, but here carrying the C45F Viceroy (244/139). Registered WGM 43K it was new to Central SMT (C43) in 1972, and acquired by Shalder in 1978 and lasted until 1983. It is seen in the second view after being donated to the Shetland Aid Appeal for help for Albania - note the 'roof box'.*

Centre Left: *The sister coach to WGM 43K was obtained in 1979, again from Central SMT (C44). WGM 44K was another YRQ (2T472457) and had the same Viceroy body (244/140), but it eventually went to Shalder on Orkney in 1987.*

Below: *Another acquisition from Central SMT (BL339) in 1979, was this 1967 Bristol Lodekka (FLF66236112) with an ECW H78F double deck body (16676) seen here at Lerwick. Donated to Ethiopia in 1987, this was probably the furthest travelled distance by any bus from Shetland, unless (of course) you know differently?*

Above: *The next member of the Shalder fleet was XMS 295K, a little Bedford J2SZ10 (IT186325) with a Plaxton Embassy B20F (728026) body. Despite being bodied by Plaxton in 1972, this design really dated from the early-1960s, and it did not compare favourably against the Duple offerings of the same period. The combination of dated body and bus-type seats can have done little to endear it to the passengers it carried over the years. Like the acquisitions on the page opposite, this little bus was purchased to strengthen the Shalder fleet in 1978, when it was bought from Knight of Kilsyth. It did not last long however, and was sold to the SIC on Whalsay two years later.*

Centre Right: *A really odd acquisition in 1980 was the 22-year old Bedford SBG (60893) with the Duple Super Vega body (1090/247) which was purchased from Bob Smith when he closed down his business at Ollaberry. Not only was it an old vehicle to acquire, but it was to last with Shalder until 1992 - a period of 12 years. I think it was intended for preservation with this firm, and it stood in the garage for a long time after it was taken off the road. At the age of 34-years it was finally sold for preservation to Moore-Style of Didsbury in 1992. Here 399 ETB stands outside Whiteness School awaiting children.*

Bottom Right: *Here we show LPS 850V, Shalder's first brand new Volvo passing John Leask & Son's office on the Esplanade in Lerwick. It had the B58-56 chassis (14238) and carried the Plaxton Supreme IV C53F body (7911VX509). It arrived with Shalder in October 1979 and was still with the fleet when it was acquired by Rapson on 1st May 1999.*

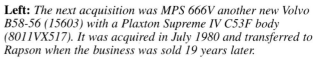

Left: *The next acquisition was MPS 666V another new Volvo B58-56 (15603) with a Plaxton Supreme IV C53F body (8011VX517). It was acquired in July 1980 and transferred to Rapson when the business was sold 19 years later.*

Right: *In August 1980 yet another Volvo B58-56 (15599) arrived, but this time sporting a Duple Dominant II 53-seat body (048/6071). It came as MPS 970W but was later re-registered FSU 718 and passed on to Rapson in 1999. It is seen here at the old bus stand in Lerwick.*

Left: *Another member of the Shalder fleet that still exists in a derelict state on Mainland Shetland at the end of 2000 is GUP 860C. Purchased from Halcrow of Burra Isle in July 1980, this Bedford VAS1 (1930) dated from 1965, and was fitted with a Duple Bella Vista C29F body (1184/30). This body was built just six weeks before our own Bella Vista (BJX 848C), and it came to Shetland from Excelsior of Dinnington in November 1976. Shalder kept this coach until 1989, at which time it was sold for a summer house. It was never re-painted in the Shalder livery, and it still remains in the orange and cream paint at the time of writing.*

Right: *Shalder's next purchase came in 1982 with OPS 899X, another new Volvo B58-56 (16364). This time it was fitted with the new Duple Dominant III body (149/6052), which had the high, raked windows that gave it an 'American Greyhound Bus' look. It remained in the fleet until February 1987, when it was sold to a company on the British mainland, but in April 1987 it was re-purchased and stayed in the fleet until the Rapson takeover. However its days were numbered by that time and it was scrapped later in 1999.*

Left: *A return to second-hand acquisitions came in 1982 when Shalder purchased PPW 847M, an eight-year old Bedford YRT (CW458097) from Sullom Voe Engineering. Fitted with a Duple Dominant C53F body (417/3034), it was to do ten years service with the Scalloway firm before being scrapped in 1992.*

Right: *The next coach, PGM 638H, was also second-hand. This was Pat Isbister's 1970 Bedford VAM70 (OT477531), with a 45-seat Duple Viceroy body (211/30). It was acquired in 1982 and later scrapped, but I do not have a precise date for this. Note the black and white liveried Volkswagen mini-bus in the background as it stands outside the garage.*

Left: *Next would come a trio of coaches ordered new by Wallace Arnold in 1975. The first of these was Leyland Leopard (PSU3C/4R7 501743) with a Plaxton Elite IV C53F body (7511LC008). HWU 58N came from an operator in North London, and would be sold to Rennie of Dunfermline in 1986.*

Right: *The second coach to come from this large tour operator was HWU 64N another Leyland Leopard (PSU3C/4R7 500248) with a Plaxton Elite IV C53F body (7511LC015). It was purchased from A.H. of Leeds in 1983 and also went to Rennie of Dunfermline in 1986. Ironically Don Spriggs of Dewsbury, a relief summertime driver for Wallace Arnold recalls that he actually brought this coach all the way to Shetland on a tour in the mid-1970s when it was relatively new. It is seen at the Scalloway garage just after coming back from a service to Walls.*

Left: *The last of the three Leyland Leopard (PSU3C/4R7 501084) had an identical Plaxton Elite IV C53F body (7511LC022) and was registered HWU 71N. It was acquired direct from Wallace Arnold in Leeds in 1983. Don Spriggs suggests that all three coaches may well have still been owned by Wallace Arnold at this time, with the earlier two merely 'on hire'. Whatever the case, it was certainly unusual to see three almost identical second-hand vehicles arrive with one Shetland operator at the same time. It was also unusual to see all three go to the same buyer when sold in 1986.*

Right: *We have seen WRN 802V before, albeit in a slightly different livery, as this mini-bus was pictured on page 29 where we examined the fleet of R. Robertson from Ulsta on Yell. This Ford Transit (PDVPWJ428890) had a Dormobile 16-seat body (3746) and dated from 1980. It was acquired by Shalder in August 1984 after Robertson lost his school contract. The Transit was later scrapped at Scalloway, although once again the date for this has eluded me thus far.*

Above: *In 1984 Shalder Coaches expanded into Orkney, when they obtained a number of contracts for school runs. As a result they purchased two vehicles from J.D. Peace, the first of which was WDU 693S. This was a Volvo B58-56 (8514) from 1977, with a 53-seat Caetano Moseley Continental Lisboa II (78060). It was acquired on 1st August 1984 and was scrapped in 1999. It is seen here parked in St. Olafs Street, Lerwick, on the Walls service some time before it was re-registered FSU 331 in 1987.*

Centre Left: *The next acquisition from Peace, also in August 1984, was OWT 1M (which would later be re-registered FSU 330 in 1987). This was a Volvo B58-56 (4867) from 1974, which had a Duple Dominant C53F body (4746751). It lasted with Shalder until 1992 when it was scrapped at Scalloway.*

Bottom Left: *Another Duple Dominant (NLS 256P) arrived in August 1987 from Rennie of Dunfermline. This was a Bedford SB5 (DW456948), it had a 41-seat body (514/1451) and dated from 1976. It lasted with Shalder until 1992 after which time it went to Romania. The SB chassis from Bedford was, by this time, some 26 years old; it had been introduced at the Commercial Motor Show in the autumn of 1950, and generally released in 1951. The SB chassis continued to be one of the most successful bus and coach chassis ever built, although it underwent progressive refinements over the years, and many examples have been seen in this book. This SB5 represents the final stages of development, and looks very stylish with the Dominant body. However, for the majority of operators it was the reliability and economy of operation that endeared them to the SB.*

Top Right: *In February 1987 Shalder purchased this Volvo B58-61 (16173) with an Irizar C45F body (3497). This 1981-built coach was originally registered LAJ 999W and came from Dales of London SE14. In 1987 it was re-registered FSU 330 and sold to Cumbria Coaches of Carlisle in March 1988.*

Centre Right: *Here we have another view of FSU 330 in Norway passing through the remains of a deep snow drift in June 1986.*

Below: *We have previously mentioned that OPS 899X was sold in February 1987, but it was re-purchased just a mere two months after being traded-in. When it came back to Scalloway it was returned in a brand new livery, with side stripes to match the rake of the windows. This vehicle would then continue to run for Shalder for 13 years before eventually being withdrawn towards the end of 1999 and scrapped earlier this year.*

Left: *Acquired from McPhillips of Armadale in April 1987, RNP 957P was a Volvo B58-56 (7667) with a Plaxton Supreme body (7511VX505). The 53-seat coach is seen here outside the garage at Scalloway and it lasted in the fleet to be acquired by Rapsons in May 1999. When this vehicle arrived in Shetland it was accompanied on the same boat by OPS 899X and D660 XPS.*

Right: *Another of those arrivals in April 1987 was the new Volvo B10M-61 (13654) registered D660 XPS. This new Volvo had the Duple 320 C53F body (8896/0362), and it too would last down into Rapson ownership in 1999. It is seen here leaving Lerwick pier loaded with tourists from a cruise liner.*

Left: *This Bedford VAS5 (EW452904) has the small 29-seat Duple Dominant body (511/1001) and dates from March 1975. It was purchased from Glenalmond College in September 1987 and, as can be seen here, HNT 945N continued doing school work in Shetland until it was withdrawn and scrapped in 1993.*

Right: *The next purchase was MGG 396P, a 1976 Bedford YRQ (EW450261), which had a 45-seat Duple Dominant body (516/2203). It was obtained from Leask's of Lerwick in April 1987 and was scrapped some 10 years later.*

Left: *Previously registered KEG 771L, 719 CEL was a 1973 Volvo B58-56 (4379) with a Plaxton Panorama Elite C53F body (733901). It was acquired from Bagnall of Swadlingcote in 1987 and it was also scrapped after 10 years service.*

Right: *Another re-registered vehicle was 64 XYD, formerly PJM 409L, once again a Volvo B58-56 with a Plaxton Panorama Elite II C53F body. As will be seen from the chassis number (4377) and the body number (733920), it was a contemporary of KEG 771L in a number of ways and the two probably went through both the Volvo factory and the Plaxton works at the same time. It came from Walters of Newport in 1987 and was scrapped in 1996.*

Left: *Moving into 1988, Shalder obtained PDO 639M, another Volvo B58-56 (4545) with a Duple Dominant C53F (474/6750). Dating from 1974, it was purchased from Gray of Killin in 1988 and finally scrapped in 1993. It is seen here on a glorious Shetland day whilst waiting at the Toft ferry terminal. The small boy in the door is Christopher Grieves, son of the Scottish transport historian Robert Grieves from Paisley.*

Right: *Also in 1988 came D31 XSS, a one year old MCW MF150/10 (MB9031), which came from Grampian (31). It stayed with Shalder for the rest of its working life and transferred to the Rapson fleet in 1999.*

Left: *In 1988 Shalder received LPS 210T, a Bedford YLQ (JW452395) from Bolts Coaches. Fitted with a Duple Dominant II C45F body (915/2143), it dated from 1979 and was another of the vehicles that passed into Shalder ownership when they bought out Bolts Coaches. Also purchased from Bolts at the same time were HAY 777L, a Bedford YRQ (CW452172) and VBM 718W, a DAF MB200DKTL (600196021). Neither of these vehicles were operated by Shalder.*

Right: *Again from Bolts of Lerwick in 1988 was A416 SPS, a Bedford YNT (DT100792), this coach featured a Plaxton Paramount C53F body (8311NTP1C026). This 1984-built vehicle was later transferred to Shalder's depot in Orkney. It is seen here with Andrew Morrison, (one of the founders) at the wheel.*

Above: *Also from the Bolts fleet came A106 MAC, a 1984 Bedford YNT (ET103969). It had the Plaxton Paramount C53F body (8411NTP1C092). It too would be transferred to the Shalder operation in Orkney not long after it's acquisition from Bolts Coaches.*

Centre Left: *Never repainted into the Shalder livery, XWK 17X retains the paint scheme in which it was received from Bolts in 1988. This Bedford YNT (LW452505) has the Plaxton Supreme V C53F body (8211NTS5C008). When it was acquired as part of the Bolts business it was not really needed by Shalder and was only operated for a few weeks before being sold to Plaxton in Anston.*

Bottom Left: *NPS 256W was a Bedford YLQ (KW455139) with a Duple Dominant II C39F body (116/2205). It was built in 1981 and formerly worked for the Shetland Islands Council. However, following a change of policy, the service was contracted out to a private operator and the vehicles sold to them to be worked on behalf of the SIC. The contract for this work changed at various times, and NPS 256W was scrapped in 1988.*

Top Right: *Here we see A343 SPS awaiting bird watchers who will be returning from the island of Mousa to the pier at Sandwick. This 18-seat coach was an Iveco-Fiat FT60/10 (10350018) with a Caetano Beja body (182160). It came from Bolts of Lerwick in 1988 when Shalder acquired that business, and in turn passed into the ownership of Rapsons in 1999.*

Centre right: *Yet another of the vehicles to be obtained from Bolts was a Bedford YLQ (JW458140) with a Duple Dominant C45 body (016/2251). Dating from 1979, LPS 963V was charitably donated to the Shetland Aids Trust in 1999.*

Below: *At 16-years old, HOR 322L was already a little long in the tooth when it came from Bolts Coaches in 1988, however, it was to last in the Shalder fleet for a further five years until it was sold to J Smith to convert into a mobile home. He had the idea that he would take it to China, but I am not really sure if he ever made it. It was a Bedford YRQ (2DZ0/2T473649), and had a Plaxton Panorama C45F body (728358).*

Left: *Again coming from Bolts in Lerwick, OPS 465X was a Ford Transit (BDVPAT440170). Dating from 1982 it had a Dormobile C16F body (9120) and lasted in the Shalder fleet until 1997 when it was scrapped.*

Right: *In this final picture of the coaches acquired from Bolts in 1988, we see a picture of USE 500R. This Duple Dominant (717/2358) had 53-seats and dated from 1977, and was scrapped at the age of 20-years in 1997. It was built on a Bedford YMT chassis (GW450618).*

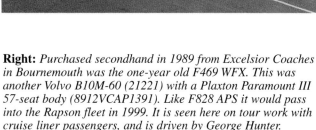

Left: *In 1989 Shalder obtained it's first new coach since D660 XPS in 1987. This was F828 APS a Volvo B10M-60 (21437) with a Plaxton Paramount III C53F body (8912VCAP1076). It had a few extra refinements and was fitted with a toilet, television and coffee machine.*

Right: *Purchased secondhand in 1989 from Excelsior Coaches in Bournemouth was the one-year old F469 WFX. This was another Volvo B10M-60 (21221) with a Plaxton Paramount III 57-seat body (8912VCAP1391). Like F828 APS it would pass into the Rapson fleet in 1999. It is seen here on tour work with cruise liner passengers, and is driven by George Hunter.*

Left: *Here we see E593 UHS, a Volvo BM10-46 (16391). This was a 38-seat Plaxton Paramount II (8895VNP3C001), which was fitted with a toilet. It was also a one-year old vehicle when acquired from Park of Hamilton in 1989, and lasted with Shalder until 1995 when it was sold to Berkeley, Paulton.*

Right: *Towards the end of the 1980s Shalder began to increase it's service bus fleet, and started to acquire a number of Talbot Pullman 22-seat buses. Here we see the first of these, E566 MAC, which had chassis number 443455, and body number 84. It was acquired as a two-year old vehicle from Roberts, Deiniolen. It was used for 6 years in Shetland before being transferred to the Orkney depot in 1996.*

Left: *Another Talbot (417184) was purchased from Dobson, Lostock, Gralem in 1989. It lasted until 1996 when it was scrapped. Registered E568 MAC it had body number 81.*

Right: *As a change from the Talbots we now show PPP 139R, a Bedford YLQ (2DZ0/FW454678). It had a Duple Dominant C45 body (815/2061) and dated from 1976. It was obtained in 1984 from J.D. Peace and was employed at Shalder's Orkney depot until 1990. It was then transferred to Scalloway where it worked for a further seven years, until scrapping took place in 1997.*

Left: *The third Talbot (430978) to be purchased was E630 MAC, and it too had the Talbot Express 22-seat body (TB182). It was obtained from Peugeot Talbot of Ryton in 1991 and lasted with Shalder until 1999 when it was scrapped.*

Right: *The final Talbot Pullman (573799), with body TB352 came from Mitchell of Plean in 1991. The twin rear axled bus, F938 TVC, lasted until 1999 when it was sold to a person in Nottingham for conversion to a caravanette.*

Above: *New to Shalder in 1990 was H410 DPS, which is pictured here with the Hillswick service at the Shalder stand in Lerwick. This Volvo B10M-60 (22687), has the Plaxton Paramount 3200 C57F body (8912VCA1702). It was also one of the vehicles to be taken over by Rapsons in May 1999.*

Centre Left: *A similar coach, J75 FPS, was acquired new in 1991. It had the Volvo chassis number 22688 and the Plaxton body number 8912VCA1704. Once again seen in Lerwick on the Scalloway service, this was another vehicle to be handed over to Rapson when they purchased the Shalder business.*

Bottom Left: *Purchased from Monet Grange of Nottingham in 1993 was the 3-year old G192 SCH. This was a MCW MF154-2 (MB9553), with a MCW Metro-Ryder C28F body. It was transferred to Orkney in 1995.*

Top Right: *Dating from 1986, D181 TSB was a Volvo B10M-61 (12416) with a Plaxton Paramount II C57F body (8712VUP3C004). It was purchased from West Coast Motors of Campbeltown in 1993 and would transfer to Rapson ownership in 1999.*

Centre Right: *In 1993 my firm of R.G. Jamieson & Son sold Shalder E609 YPS, a Mercedes 811D (670303-20-851692). It had a Reeve Burgess C29F body (16919) which dated from 1988. It remained in the Shalder fleet until 1999 but was scrapped following an accident. This came about after the coach was blown over during a severe gale whilst it was returning from a school run to Burra Isle. Fortunately it was empty at the time and the driver walked away unscathed.*

Below: *Another acquisition from a Shetland operator was KPS 701T, a Bedford YLQ (JW451717). Coming from John Leask & Sons in 1993, this coach had a Plaxton Supreme 45-seat body (7910QX503). It is seen here in the winter of 1993/1994 standing at the depot after being on a school run. It had been painted into the newer style Shalder livery but would remain in Shetland for only a short period of time, and was transferred to Orkney in 1994.*

Above: *Obtained from John G. Gordon of Dornoch in 1994, we see D982 NJS at Shalder's Brae depot. This Mercedes 609D (668063-20781768), had a Dixon Lumax C27F body. It dated from 1987, and entered the Rapson fleet in 1999.*

Centre Left: *The well known company, Mayne of Buckie, supplied FUJ 905V, a Bedford YMT (KW450681) to Shalder in 1994. The Duple Dominant C53F (017/2509) dated from 1980 and is seen here in it's un-repainted form. It went to Rapson in May 1999 but was given to the Romania Appeal in December.*

Bottom Left: *Dating from 1976 GBS 714P was a Bedford YRQ (EW454232) with a Duple Dominant C45F body (616/2200). It came from J.D. Peace of Orkney in 1997, but went back to Shalder's depot in Orkney the following year.*

Bottom Right: *Dating from 1987 this Ford Transit (BDVWHK69821) has a Mellor C16F body (52368). Purchased from Herbert Nicolson of Bixter in 1997, E974 MSE did not last in the Shalder fleet for very long and was scrapped in 1999.*

Top Left: *Another transfer from the Orkney depot was C771 FBH, a Bedford YNT (FT700400) which dated from 1985. It had the Duple 320 C53F body (8592/9255) and came from Orkney in 1997 but was soon returned there.*

Top Right : *On hire for a period of three months during 1997, G639 BHP was a Talbot Pullman (430119) with a 20-seat bus body (168). This 1989-built, came from and was returned to the Talbot factory and was never painted in Shalder colours.*

Centre Right Bottom: *The last new vehicles bought by Shalder came in 1998 and were a pair of MAN 11.220s, with Marshall B36 bodies. The chassis serial numbers were WNA469238 9G115937 on S388 JPS and WNA469238 7G115892 on S389 JPS; the body numbers were 032 and 033 respectively. After the take-over Rapsons did not think these vehicles were needed in Shetland and duly transferred them to their depot in Inverness.*

Below: *As stated earlier, E609 YPS had been written off, but a replacement was quickly obtained in the form of Panther Travel's G110 DSG. This Mercedes 814D (67031320943816) had a Reeve Burgess C33F body (17734) new in 1989, and it stayed with Shalder into Rapson ownership.*

In a fleet as large as that operated by Shalder, it is inevitable that many changes would occur over the years. Most notable were the paint-work changes, such as the striking 'banded' livery that replaced the simple black and white scheme of the early years. Other changes were re-registrations, which came into vogue in the 1980s, when 'cherished' number plates became fashionable. The pictures on this page reflect these changes, but specific vehicle details are not recorded, as these have already been discussed on the preceding pages.

Top Left: *First we see LPS 850V with a paint scheme change.*

Top Right: *FSU 330 is a registration plate change for OWT 1M, although one would have thought that the former number was valuable enough to become a 'cherished plate' in its own right.*

Centre Left Top: *Next came MPS 666V, another paint change.*

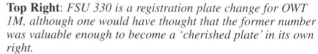

Centre Left Bottom: *The third vehicle to carry the plate FSU 331 (WDU 639S), is seen at Lerwick after a re-paint and registration plate change.*

Bottom Left: *Next we show RNP 957P after being re-liveried.*

Bottom Right: *Finally we have a picture of MPS 970W following complete rebuild, re-paint and a registration change to FSU 718.*

THE RAPSON GROUP

A new operator to Shetland, is the Rapson Group who acquired Shalder Coaches in May 1999. This progressive company has acquired a number of Scottish operators in recent years, and obviously saw an opportunity to expand into Shetland and Orkney. It's stylish two-tone blue livery has since been progressively applied to the coaches taken over (and retained) from the Shalder operation. Although Rapson have only operated for six months in the 20th-Century, they have made quite an impact and decidedly taken the former Shalder operation into the 21st-Century. With around two dozen vehicles in the fleet, operating on a mixture of public service, private hire and school work in Shetland, plus those based in Orkney, this will be an operation to watch in the future.

Above: *Wearing the new Rapson style two-tone blue livery, but still showing the Shalder name we see a pair of Bedford YNTs that were brought from Shalder Coaches in Orkney shortly after the takeover. However, the new bird logo (Rapson's soaring eagle) is obviously at variance from the oyster catcher that gave Shalder their name. Full details on THB 420Y and THB 424Y are given on pages 92 and 93.*

Centre Right: *Another repaint job is seen on G110 GSG, which is the Mercedes 814D seen on page 89 in the all white Panther livery. This vehicle was obtained by Shalder not long before the takeover, from Stevens of Birmingham (Panther).*

Bottom Right: *A number of vehicles were transferred between the Shetland and Orkney depots after the takeover, including JIL 5809. This was a Bedford YMP (DT103719) with a Plaxton Paramount body (831DMQP1C003). Dating from 1983 this vehicle had originally been registered XVN 501Y, and had 45-seats.*

The vehicles that Rapsons took over from Shalder included:-

Reg.	Chassis	Body	Cap.	Year	Acq.
LPS 850V	Volvo B58-56	Plaxton	C53F	1979	1999
MPS 666V	Volvo B58-56	Plaxton	C53F	1980	1999
FSU 718	Volvo B58-56	Duple	C53F	1980	1999
OPS 899X	Volvo B58-56	Duple	C53F	1982	1999
FSU 331	Volvo B58-56	Caetano	C53F	1984	1999
RNP 597P	Volvo B58-56	Plaxton	C53F	1976	1999
D660 XPS	Volvo B10M-61	Duple	C53F	1987	1999
D31 XSS	MCW MF150/10	MCW	C25F	1987	1999
LPS 210T	Bedford YLQ	Duple	C45F	1979	1999
A343 SPS	Iveco-Fiat	Caetano	C18F	1983	1999
LPS 963V	Bedford YLQ	Duple	C45F	1979	1999
F828 APS	Volvo B10M/60	Plaxton	C53F	1989	1999
F469 WFX	Volvo B10M/60	Plaxton	C57F	1988	1999
E630 MAC	Talbot	Pullman	B22F	1988	1999
F938 TVC	Talbot	Pullman	B22F	1989	1999
H410 DPS	Volvo B10M/60	Plaxton	C57F	1990	1999
J75 FPS	Volvo B10M/60	Plaxton	C57F	1991	1999
D181 TSB	Volvo B10M/61	Plaxton	C57F	1986	1999
D982 NJS	Mercedes 609D	Dixon	C27F	1987	1999
FUJ 905V	Bedford YMT	Duple	C53F	1980	1999
S388 JPS	MAN 11.22	Marshall	B36F	1998	1999
S389 JPS	MAN 11.22	Marshall	B36F	1998	1999

Top Left: *As noted earlier the condition of the purchase of Shalder Coaches was that Andrew Morrison (one of the partners), should also give up his own independent operation in which P10 ASM was employed as the sole vehicle. This Marshall SLF (SMVFBL1R KTC105089), with it's C26F body thus joined the Rapson fleet, but at first it retained it's red paint scheme and gained a Shalder badge.*

Centre Left Top: *D982 NJS is another of the vehicles acquired from Shalder Coaches, full details being given on page 88, where it is shown in the livery of John G. Gordon.*

Centre Left Bottom: *Obtained from Western (fleet number 068), H180 GTA was a Mercedes 609D (6703032P081661). It has a Carlyle B29F body (C19.190) and dates from 1991.*

Bottom Left: *Shortly after the takeover a pair of Bedford YNTs were transferred from Shalder Coaches in Orkney. The first of these had chassis number DT104009; it carried the Plaxton Paramount C53F body (8311NTPIC032) and the registration plate THB 420Y.*

Bottom Right: *The second Bedford coach to be brought to Shetland by Rapsons was THB 424Y, and it was almost identical to THB 420Y. It had chassis number DT104029, and the Plaxton body number 8311NTPIC033.*

Above: *This Volvo B10BLE (YV3R4A514TA002921) with an Alexander ALX300 B44F body (9806/4) was new in August 1998. Registered S376 MVP this bus was sent to work with Rapson as a demonstrator in the summer of 1999. It remained at Scalloway for around three months before being returned to the manufacturers.*

The vehicles acquired by Rapsons after the takeover from Shalder included the following list up to 31st December 1999:

Reg.	Chassis	Body	Cap.	Year	Acq.
THB 420Y	Bedford YNT	Plaxton	C53F	1983	1999
THB 424Y	Bedford YNT	Plaxton	C53F	1983	1999
JIL 5809	Bedford YMP	Plaxton	C45F	1983	1999
P10 ASM	Marshall SLF	Marshall	C27F	1997	1999
H180 GTA	Mercedes 609D	Carlyle	B29F	1991	1999

Centre Right: *Purchased new in May 1999, T134 AST is a Volvo B6BLE (YV3R3A917XCO10020) with a Wright Crusader B37F body (B12). It carries Rapson's Highland Livery with an eagle pictured on the side. The two-tone blue paint scheme would later be applied to the former Shalder vehicles that passed to Rapsons, but the Shalder name would replace the Highland lettering.*

Bottom Right: *V32 JST carries the new Shalder livery on this Volvo B6BLE (YV3R3A912XCO10071) with a Wright Crusader B37F body (B418). New in September 1999, it is seen leaving the Viking Bus Station in Lerwick on the service to Walls; standing alongside is John White's Mercedes 711D, N762 KPS.*

HALCROW

Separated from the Mainland for centuries by Cliff Sound, the main crossing to Burra Isle was by a ferry called the *Tirrick* (the Shetland name for the tern). A bus service for school children on the island was provided under contract by Erasmus Duncan Halcrow (known locally as Raffie). Older children going to school would take the bus to the *Tirrick*, which was operated by Hance Smith. He provided this vital service until a new road bridge system was completed in 1971, linking Burra Isle and Trondra with the Mainland. Thereafter road transport was used to take children to school in Scalloway and Raffie continued to provide this service until the contract passed to Shalder in 1980.

Below: *To fulfil his school contracts Halcrow purchased ADY 576B, which is pictured here. This Bedford J2LZ has a Duple Compact B19F body, and dated from 1964. It carried on the work from the summer of 1971 until it was scrapped in 1976.*

Above: *The J2 was then supplemented by the Sunderland-registered GUP 860C, a Bedford VAS1 (1930) with a Duple Bella Vista C29F body (11/8430). Dating from 1965, the coach (picture above) was purchased in November 1972 from Excelsior Coaches of Dinnington. The VAS1 was sold to Shalder Coaches in 1980, but it still remains (in a derelict state) after being sold for use as a greenhouse.*

CECIL SLATER

Based at Tingwall Cecil Slater is well known to generations of local school children, as he has been doing school contract work for twenty years or more. Initially this was done with vehicles having small seating capacity, but in September 1995 he acquired N569 JHS a 16-seat LDV 400 (SEYZMYSFACN965147). As seen above, this vehicle has an LDV conversion body, and it is still operating today.

For many visitors to Shetland, their first port of call will be Lerwick, as this is the terminal point for the P&O Scottish Ferries service from Aberdeen. At the time of writing this service is provided six days a week with the ro-ro ferries, *St. Clair* and *St. Sunniva*, with the *St. Rognvald* operating the freight traffic. Lerwick is taken from the Norse name Leir Vik (muddy bay), and has been a haven for sailors for many years. For example, it was here that the Norwegian King Harald Hardrada sheltered on his way south to do battle with the English King Harold at Stamford Bridge in 1066. Ever since Lerwick has been a pivotal point in Shetland's transport history, and the town has grown to become the main commercial and administrative centre for the Northern Isles. Several coach operators have been based here over the years, but the main one has to be the firm of John Leask & Son, who are now based in offices on the Esplanade.

JOHN LEASK & SON

John Leask & Son was established in 1919 as a taxi operator, by John R. Leask, who had originally worked as a coachman for Leslie of Laxfirth. In 1922 John was joined in the business by his son Jamie, and later by sons Magnus (Sonny), Freddie and Laurence (Lollie). Further details are given overleaf.

Above: *Typical of the Lerwick 'tour bus' scene in the 1950s, this view shows PS 2107, PS 1927, FBU 149, PS 2038, PS 2001, EFS 196, lined up at the town's Market Cross with adverts for various tours.*

Centre Right: *Here we see Leask's first bus, RS 5927 a 13-seat charabanc of 1923 vintage, which came to Lerwick in 1928. In the picture is the founder John Leask. We do not know precisely how long this vehicle was retained before it was finally scrapped.*

Bottom Right: *A rear view of the same bus, RS 5927, showing its name 'Lynn o' Dee' on the rear. Note the opening canvas roof, just the job for a Shetland winter!*

Top Left: *Another picture of that first bus, as John Leask is seen at the wheel of Reo RS 5927.*

Centre Left: *The second vehicle, another Reo Charabanc (RS 8023) was purchased as a 10-year old vehicle in 1934. On the back was the lettering 'Ben MacDhui'.*

Bottom Left: *Bus number three came in 1935, in the guise of a 1931 Chevrolet Duple B14, registered RM 6849. It became known as the 'Gutters Bus' owing to the short service it did between the town and the herring station at the north harbour.*

During the 1920s motorised transport around the Northern Isles (such as it was) was mainly provided with large cars with up to 7-seat bodies, but as time progressed a demand began to emerge for a greater carrying capacity. As a result the first 'proper' bus, a Reo Charabanc with 13 seats arrived in 1928.

With the arrival of these larger vehicles, the business expanded during the 1930s with a mix of private hires, summer tours and a regular service between Lerwick and Mossbank to connect with the ferry to Yell. Commencing in 1932, this operation grew to become the 'Overland Service', which of course still operates today.

The start of air travel to Shetland in 1936 opened up more opportunities with a service being operated between Lerwick and Sumburgh Airport. Leask's became the Shetland agents for Allied Airways at the time and the present travel agency side of the business evolved from that. After World War II, the year 1949 saw the start of the Lerwick Town Service using a Utility Bodied Bedford OWB registered SU 4099. Sceptics gave it six months at the time, but after 51 years it still continues to run and is well used by the public of Lerwick. In 1963 the Lerwick firm of Ganson Brothers was acquired, followed by the firm of James Johnson & Son, from Scalloway in 1968.

The discovery of oil in waters around Shetland then brought a large increase in transport requirements during the 1970s and 1980s. The fleet size gradually increased and in 1983 Leask's acquired the business of A J Eunson, Virkie, taking the fleet size to 19. The fleet today is mainly DAF, with low floor accessible buses operating on the Town Service and the run to the South Mainland. School contracts, summer tours and private hire are still operated as they have been since the early days. Over the years a sizeable fleet list has developed, and this is shown below and on the facing page:-

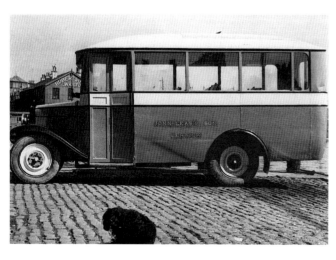

Reg.	Chassis	Body	Cap.	Year	Acq.
RS 5927	REO	Charabanc	B13	1923	1928
RS 8023	REO	Charabanc	B13	1924	1934
RM 6849	Chevrolet	Duple	B14F	1931	1935
RG 2267	Bedford WLB	Duple	C20F	1931	1936
PO 7619	Bedford WLB	Duple	C20F	1934	1937
RG 3561	Bedford WLB	Duple	C20F	1933	1939
AMS 240	Bedford OWB	SMT	B28F	1944	1944
CAV 269	Bedford OWB	SMT	B28F	1944	1945
SU 4099	Bedford OWB	Duple	B28F	1944	1948
WG 5773	Bedford WTB	Duple	C26F	1938	1948
PS 1927	Austin CBX	Kenex	C32C	1950	1950
FBU 149	Bedford OB	Plaxton	C30F	1949	1950
HGG 540	Morris	Churchill	C31F	1949	1950
SL 3474	Bedford OB	Duple	C29F	1950	1951
PS 2107	Bedford SB	Duple	C33F	1951	1951
KWX 412	Bedford SB	Duple	C33F	1951	1954
SY 9964	Bedford SB	Duple	C33F	1951	1954
PS 2627	Bedford SBG	Duple	C41F	1956	1956
DYJ 833	Bedford SBG	Duple	C38F	1955	1958
MVA 891	Bedford SBG	Duple	C41F	1955	1959
HAA 553	Leyland PSI	Duple	C35F	1949	1961
VNE 575	Bedford SB3	Duple	C41F	1958	1962
LSN 56	Bedford SB3	Duple	C41F	1960	1963
WGD 551	Bedford SB3	Duple	C41F	1959	1964
KGB 759	Bedford SB	Brush	C33F	1952	1964
SSA 550	AEC Reliance	Harrington	C37F	1960	1966
6876 SM	Bedford SB3	Plaxton	C41F	1962	1966
UWX 921	Bedford SB3	Plaxton	C41F	1958	1967
HMS 227	Bedford SB	Burlingham	C35F	1955	1968

Reg.	Chassis	Body	Cap.	Year	Acq.
951 UVT	Bedford SB5	Yeates	DP45F	1962	1969
TBU 823G	Bedford VAM70	Duple	C45F	1969	1970
BPS 987K	Bedford YRQ	Plaxton	C45F	1972	1972
XSN 44J	Ford R192	Plaxton	C45F	1971	1974
HPS 27P	Bedford YMT	Plaxton	C53F	1976	1976
GWG 481	AEC Monocoach	Alexander	B45F	1955	1975
HMS 233	AEC Reliance	Alexander	B45F	1956	1975
MGG 396P	Bedford YRQ	Duple	C45F	1976	1977
UHS 602R	Bedford YMT	Plaxton	C53F	1977	1978
KFU 867P	Bedford NJM	Plaxton	C41F	1976	1978
KPS 959T	Bedford YMT	Plaxton	C53F	1979	1979
GRS 11E	Leyland	Alexander	B43D	1967	1979
NPS 161W	Leyland Leopard	Plaxton	C53F	1981	1981
OPS 742X	Leyland Leopard	Duple	C53F	1981	1981
ORS 84H	Albion Viking	Alexander	DP28F	1970	1982
JAR 614G	AEC Reliance	Plaxton	C53F	1969	1983
PGM 639H	Bedford VAM 70	Duple	C45F	1970	1983
JPT 774N	Bedford YRQ	Plaxton	C45F	1974	1983
VYH 499M	Bedford YRQ	Plaxton	C45F	1974	1983
MPS901W	Bedford YMQ	Plaxton	C45F	1980	1983
B885 TPS	DAF SB230DHS	Plaxton	C53F	1985	1985
A801TGG	Man MT8 136	Reeve Bu	C28F	1983	1985
EBL 390K	Bristol RELL6L	ECW	DP50F	1972	1985
D353 XPS	Fiat	Caetano	C22F	1986	1987
NSA 255P	Ford R1114	Plaxton	DP58F	1976	1988
RAG 390M	Leyland Leopard	Alexander	DP49F	1974	1988
E658 YPS	DAF SB2300	Plaxton	C57F	1988	1988
D92 ALA	Fiat 35-9	Elme	C16F	1986	1988
F851 APS	DAF SB2305	Plaxton	C57F	1989	1989
G621 CPS	Dennis Javelin	Duple	B55F	1990	1990
C629 PAU	DAF MB2300K	Plaxton	C53F	1986	1990
KPS 701T	Bedford YLQ	Plaxton	C45F	1979	1991
E700YNS	Dennis Javelin	Plaxton	C35F	1988	1991
J662 FPS	DAF SB2305	Plaxton	C55F	1992	1992
K389 NGG	Ford Transit	Dormobile	C16F	1992	1992
G953 KJX	DAF SB2305	Plaxton	C57F	1990	1993
J478 XHL	Mercedes 709D	Plaxton	C25F	1991	1993
YOT 545V	Leyland National	Leyland	B44D	1980	1993
K300 CCC	Man 11-190	Caetano	C33F	1993	1994
M431 HOX	Renault	Jubilee	C14F	1994	1994
M20 JLS	DAF MB230LT	Van Hool	C57F	1995	1995
N746 LUS	LDV 400	Pearl	B20F	1995	1995
N20 JLS	DAF DE33WSS	Ikarus	C55F	1996	1996
P20 JLS	Mercedes 711D	Plaxton	C25F	1997	1997
H540 YCX	DAF SB2305	Plaxton	C55F	1991	1997
R20 JLS	DAF DE33WSS	Ikarus	C53F	1998	1998
S20 JLS	Mercedes 0814D	Plaxton	B31F	1998	1998
M833 RCP	DAF SB220	Ikarus	B48F	1995	1998
T20 JLS	DAF DEO2GS	Ikarus	B43F	1999	1999
T30 JLS	DAF DEO2GS	Ikarus	B43F	1999	1999
T40 JLS	DAF DEO2GS	Ikarus	B43F	1999	1999
T50 JLS	DAF DEO2GS	Ikarus	B43F	1999	1999

Top Right: *As will be seen from the name below the windscreen, RG 2267 (a Bedford WLB from 1931 with a Duple C20F body) was purchased from Swallow of Aberdeen in 1936. It was sold to Ganson Bros. in 1943, and shortly afterwards was requisitioned by the RAF. During this time it smashed into a road block at 'Da Lang Kames' and was badly damaged.*

Centre Right Top: *Next came PO 7619, a Bedford WLB with a 20-seat Duple body. It came from Watson of Pitlochry in 1937 and was sold to Morrison of Bigton in 1948.*

Centre Right Bottom: *Look, there was no one-way system on Commercial Street, when RG 3561 was photographed outside the Lerwick Post Office! This was a 1933 Bedford WLB (108911) with a Walker C20F body, which was bought from Hall of Aberdeen in 1939, and sold to my grandfather in 1948.*

Bottom Right: *At the time of arrival the paint work on RG 3561 was mottled in autumn colours and put on with a sponge! As a result it was called the 'Bonnie Briar Bush', and it is pictured here at Sumburgh Airport in the Leask livery.*

Left: *As will be appreciated, World War II changed the transport needs of Shetland, bringing greater demand for bus services. Vehicles were in short supply though, and Leask's were fortunate to acquire Bedford OWB (22845) AMS 240. With its SMT 28-seat body it came from Alexander's (W152) in April 1944 at just a few months old; it was sold to J.G. Hunter of Unst in 1951.*

Right: *Another 1944 OWB (18067) with a Scottish Motor Traction (SMT) body was CAV 269, which was purchased in 1945. As a point of interest the OWB was the only single-deck bus or coach that the government allowed to be built during World War II, and the internal appointments of the standard body produced by Duple, SMT and Charles Roe were frugal to say the least. CAV 269 lasted until 1951, when it was sold to Johnson's of Scalloway.*

Left: *The third OWB (11501) was SU 4099, which had a Duple B28F body. It also dated from 1944, but was not purchased until 1948, when it arrived in Lerwick from Coull of Auchinblue. By this time many mainland operators were ridding themselves of the austere OWBs, and replacing them with the new 29-seat OBs that Bedford were producing with coachbuilders like Duple, Plaxton and others. These were far better appointed than the OWBs, and even the service buses had the luxury of proper upholstered seats, as opposed to the slatted wood seats on the OWB. Before it was sold to Hunter of Nesting in 1952, SU 4099 was mostly used on the town service. From left to right we see Dennis Watt (driver) Winnie Edwardson (conductress?), and Freddie Leask.*

Right: *After the war, shortages in new bus chassis resulted in the purchase of pre-war models like this Bedford WTB (111080, with a Duple C26F body (5673). It dated from 1938 and was purchased in November 1948 from Alexander where it had fleet number W58. It remained with Leask's until March 1955, when it was sold to J.J. & A. Leslie in the South Mainland. It was no stranger to this part of Shetland, and it is seen here at Sumburgh Airport with its driver Sandy Laurenson. Note the British European Airways (BEA) sign on the right.*

Left: *A second view (this time a rear-three-quarter shot) of WG 5773 has been included, because it clearly shows that the Bedford retained the Alexander livery for some little while (note the bluebird emblem is still on the side). Again taken outside the airport, the coach would be providing the linking service to Lerwick . Note the canvas roof on the coach, which was designed to pull back and provide passengers with an open topped bus or 'sun saloon'.*

Right: *As the restrictions on new vehicle purchases eased, and manufacturers were under less obligation to produce for export. So new coaches started to become available, but even so it was still no easy matter to get the type of chassis or body you wanted. Austin was not a popular model of bus in Shetland, but it was a proud day when PS 1927 arrived at Lerwick in February 1950. This Austin CBX (143402) had a Kenex C32C body and would last with John Leask & Son until it was sold to Georgeson & Moore in 1958.*

Left: *The firm soon returned to buying Bedford, and this 1949 Plaxton-bodied (563) Bedford OB (91911) was purchased from Renton of Oldham. Just a year-old at the time, this full-front coach had 30-seats, a fact that was made possible by the use of forward control. This gave extra seating over the Duple Vista body, and thus helped bring in extra revenue. The driver in this view is Willie Peterson, who is pictured here with FBU 149 at Mavis Grind.*

Right: *Although I have tried to avoid repeating pictures of the same vehicle in this book, this view of FBU 149 simply could not be omitted. In what is a glorious period picture, the Plaxton-bodied coach is seen picking up passengers and luggage from the plane at Sumburgh Airport. The coach was retained by Leask's until 1956, when it was sold to J. G. Hunter on Unst.*

Left: *Another unusual acquisition in 1950, was HGG 540 a 1949 Morris Commercial (316) with a Churchill C31F body. This had the distinction of being the first diesel-powered bus in Shetland . However these Morris Commercials were fitted with the under-powered Saurer diesel, which were quite notorious for their poor running. The Morris came from Haldane of Glasgow in 1950, and lasted for 11 years before being scrapped in 1961.*

Right: *Once again I have repeated a picture of a bus shown before, not because the vehicle has any particular merit, but because of the setting in which it is seen. This wonderful view of 'Lerwick from the Pier' will bring back many memories for a whole lot of different reasons. As for HGG 540, it would have passed this way many times as it was latterly used on the company's 'Town Service'.*

Above: *This is yet another of those pictures that just had to be included, as it shows the vagaries of bus operation in Shetland. The 1950 Bedford OB (140027) seen here had a Duple Vista (56081) 29-seat body, and was purchased from London Scottish Alva in 1951. It was one of the last batch of OBs to be produced, and in the autumn of that year Vauxhall Motors would release their new SB coach, which was marketed as the 'Big Bedford'. In this view we see SL 3474 making heavy work on a working to Sumburgh in heavy snow, and is going via 'Da Black Gaet' to avoid the normal route through the Hill of Sound. The driver is Jamie Leask, whilst the man (on the right) wearing the cap and holding the shovel is the well known driver, Freddie Williamson.*

Bottom Left: *As mentioned earlier, the Commercial Motor Show of 1950 saw the launch of the new Bedford SB type, and at this event three SBs would be displayed. One was on the Vauxhall-Bedford stand, one was on the Duple stand, and one was used outside the show to do demonstration runs. One of these coaches was the SB that would be later registered as KWX 412 in August 1951, and would (in 1954) join the Leask fleet. However, before that event occurred, John Leask & Son purchased a brand new SB (2440) with a Duple Vega 33-seat body (56820). Registered PS 2107 it is seen here at Voe in the early 1950s, sometime before it was sold to Thomsons of Sandwick in March 1956.*

Top Right: *During the past year I have found out a great deal about KWX 412, and would especially like to thank the people at Vauxhall Motors who have been so kind in helping me to find out so much about its history. I acquired the coach over 20-years ago, at a time when it would probably have been scrapped, but I liked this Bedford SB (SBL2 - later 3743) so much, that I had the idea of preserving it. That dream is now about to be fulfilled, and soon full restoration will be commenced. As stated previously, this coach came to Leask's in 1954 from Heaps of Leeds. It had been completely refurbished in July 1951 after its days as a Vauxhall demonstrator were over, and sold to Kildare of East Ardwick. They sold the Duple Vega-bodied coach (56794) to Heaps in March 1953, and they in turn replaced the Duple service bus seats with Plaxton coach seats (which are still in it today). It is seen here in the North Mainland at Eshaness Lighthouse whilst on tour.*

Centre Right: *Another view of KWX 412 on the relatively new pier at Toft (opened in 1951) as it off-loads its cargo of passengers and mail on to the ferry* Tystic, *which will provide the next leg of the Overland Service to Yell and Unst.*

Below: *Here we see SY 9964 on the same pier at Toft, but this time collecting passengers and mail from Yell coming off the ferry boat* Shalder *(the Shetland name for the oyster catcher). This was Leask's third Duple-bodied (56963) SB (1207), and a chassis that would have been one of the early production batch from the start of 1951. It was acquired in 1954 from Hunter of Loanhead, and stayed in service until 1966, when it was sold to Georgeson & Moore in Scalloway. As will be seen in this evocative picture, the Vega body had the optional roof cant rail windows, which added significantly to the cost of the vehicle when new. The driver here was Freddie Williamson, who was taking a private hire for the Ian Powrie Scottish Dance Band and the famous singer Andy Stewart. The skipper of the ferry, Robbie Jarmson, is seen at the front of the boat, whilst his crewman (Peter Arthur) watches with his hands in his pockets.*

Left: *A typical feature of Leask's work, at least during the summer months, were the tours that the company operated from Lerwick's Market Cross. Here we show a picture that represents this work, as a Bedford SB-Duple Vega (SY 9964), stands waiting to pick up passengers for a 'Circular Tour'. As will be seen from the advertising board, the tour started at 2.15pm, and returned at 6.15pm. The tour ran via Tingwall, Voe, Dales Lees, Sullom Voe, Mavis Grind, Brae, Kergord, Weisdale, Scalloway (stop for tea at the Scalloway Hotel) and finally returned via the Tingwall Valley. The trip cost the grand sum of six shillings!*

Right: *A development of the SB came in the mid-1950s with the Bedford SBG, and when this was coupled to the superbly stylish Duple Super Vega body it was a winning combination. In May 1956 the company purchased one of these SBGs (44895) with the 'Butterfly Grill' Super Vega body (1060/388) brand new. Registered PS 2627 it is seen here climbing the hill at Firth near Mossbank. The 41-seat coach was sold to Johnson of Scalloway in 1964, and despite being heavily worked in the years that followed, its remains are still on the Shetland Mainland.*

Left: *Leask's so liked the Super Vega, that they went on to purchase a number of second-hand examples when they became available. The first of these was DYJ 833 with a 38-seat body (1055/215), which had the chassis number 35441 and dated from 1955. It was purchased from Dicksons of Dundee in 1958, and sold on to Georgeson & Moore in 1964. The proud-looking driver DYJ 883 on this occasion was Tammie Tulloch.*

Right: *Next came MVA 891, which had chassis 43090 and body 1060/128. It was new in 1955 and came as a four-year old vehicle from Spence on Orkney. It is pictured here in happy times, as it prepares to leave Lerwick on the Overland Saturday return service during the summer months. Sadly the coach was later destroyed in a gale and completely written-off!*

Left: *I said that MVA 891 was destroyed in a storm, but that is quite an understatement, as the SBG got blown off the road and down a hill towards the cliffs at Cunningsburgh during a tremendous gale in 1967. The Super Vega body was blown right over, and was totally wrecked as this remarkable picture dramatically reveals. Quite incredibly (considering the devastation) the driver, Sidney Hepburn, was only bruised. Fortunately, as the coach began to roll over, he managed to wedge himself under the dashboard and this act of 'quick-thinking' undoubtedly saved his life.*

Right: *In between the Super Vega coaches that they used on work like the tours and the Overland Service, John Leask & Son purchased a Leyland PS1 (473350) predominantly for its services around Lerwick. This 1949 half-cab was fitted with a 35-seat Duple body (45884), and was purchased from McLennan of Spittalfield in 1961. Quite a sizeable bus for Shetland, this Leyland was registered HAA 553 and is seen here on the town service. It lasted with the company until 1969 when it was eventually scrapped.*

Left: *The final SBG (59800) with a 'Butterfly Grill) Super Vega body (1090/164) to be purchased, VNE 575, came from Manchester Motors in 1962. This 1958-built coach lasted with Leask's until 1966 when it went to Johnson of Scalloway. It is pictured here at Sumburgh Airport in the early 1960s, with a Lomas-bodied ambulance behind.*

Right: *The development of the Super Vega body was the really stylish Duple Super Vega II, an exceptionally attractive coach that took the coaching world by storm at the end of the 1950s. In March 1963 one of these 41-seat bodies (1120/283) on a Bedford SB3 chassis (75428) was purchased from Elliot's of Jamestown. Registered LSN 56 in 1960, it is seen here at Market Cross, Lerwick, complete with the orange sun visor at the front. This coach would remain with Leask's until 1978, before it was sold on to Johnson Bros., Brae.*

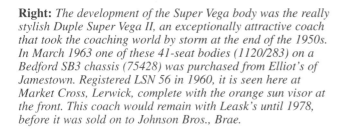

Left: *A similar SB3 (68733), dating from 1959 was purchased from Haldane of Glasgow in 1964. It was sold to H. Sinclair on Yell in 1976, and was eventually withdrawn from service and sold to a house-owner in the village of West Sandwick who used it as a greenhouse. The Super Vega II (1105/304) stood outside this property, gradually deteriorating until the summer of 2000, when it was cut up and taken away by the Shetland Amenity Trust. It is shown in happier times outside John Leask & Sons' office before heading for the airport on hire to BEA.*

Right: *With the two Super Vega II coaches in the fleet, Leask's were ready to use these on the summer tour work, as they certainly provided a comfortable ride. Both coaches also had the added luxury of the roof cant rail windows and front roof windows. There were slight livery differences and WGD 551 featured a blue roof, whilst that on LSN 56 was cream. The two are seen here at the Market Cross plying for tourists.*

Opposite Page Top: *As we have shown, Leask's operated a number of early Bedford SBs, but by 1964 only SY 9964 was still in the fleet, both PS 2107 and KWX 412 having already departed. However, when the Lerwick firm of Ganson Brothers was bought out by Leask's, another SB (1094) was to join SY 9964. This was KGB 759 a Brush-bodied (101) SB. Although this coach looked very much like the Duple Vega, it was in fact built at Loughborough in 1952 at a time when Duple were having production problems. A strike, a new body design, and a continuing demand for new coaches combined to create difficulties for the Hendon management team. According to Marc Thomas from Leicester (who worked for Brush), his firm had spare capacity at the time and were allowed to build a number of Vega-style coaches under licence from Duple. There were a number of styling differences, notably in the windows, but the overall appearance was the same. KGB 759 remained with Leask & Sons until 1969, at which time it was sold to J.W. Laurenson on Unst.*

Opposite Bottom: *The stylish designs of Sussex coach-builder, Thomas Harrington were not that common in Shetland, so when SSA 550 appeared at Lerwick in October 1966 it must have caused something of a stir. This was an AEC Reliance 470 (2MU3RA2925) with a Harrington Cavalier C37F body (2219), which was new in April 1960. Purchased from McIntyre of Bucksburn, the coach is seen on the quay at Lerwick. It would do some 14-years service with Leask's before being scrapped in 1980.*

Top Right: *As previously discussed the Market Cross in Lerwick was the starting point for many of the Tour Services operated in Shetland. In this 1961 picture we see Leask's DYJ 833, Ganson's KGB 66 and KGB 759, and Leask's MVA 891, and PS 2627.*

Centre Right Top: *In a view from a different angle, we see tour buses at the Market Cross in 1963; these are all owned by John Leask & Son, and include LSN 56, PS 2627, MVA 891.*

Centre Right Bottom: *The Scarborough coach-builder Plaxton had not been well represented in the early Leask fleet list, but two such bodied coaches were to be purchased in the mid-1960s. The first of these was 6876 SM, a Bedford SB3 (89150) with a Plaxton Embassy body (622897). This C41F came from Little's of Annan in October 1966, and lasted until July 1979 before being sold on to Sinclair of West Sandwick. Carrying a Dumfriesshire registration plate, the coach is seen here at Sumburgh Airport.*

Bottom Right: *Registered in the West Riding of Yorkshire in 1958, was this SB3 (60381) which is shown at the Toft ferry terminal. UWX 921 was a Plaxton Consort C41F (2179), which was purchased from Shankland of Carlisle in 1967, and sold to Miller Construction in 1974. Its role as a worker's bus was not a long one, and the vehicle was scrapped in 1975.*

Above: *As the Burlingham Seagull and Baby Seagull are my publisher's favourite coaches, I was not surprised to see that he had decided to use this picture of HMS 227 in as large a format as possible. Dating from 1955 the Bedford SB (47018), had the front entrance 35-seat Burlingham body (6307). It was new to Alexander, and worked in their Northern fleet as NW260 before being sold to Leask's in 1968. It remained with this company until 1974, when it was sold to Johnson Bros. in Brae.*

Centre Left Top: *Very few Yeates bodied buses have survived into preservation, which thus makes 951 UVT a very rare survivor. This is another of the vehicles that still survive in Shetland and is the subject of a preservation attempt at the time of writing. This forward control Bedford SB5 (89325) had a specially lengthened chassis at the front, thus allowing the driving position and entry doors to be ahead of the front axle. Supplied new to Potteries Motor Traction in 1962 (fleet number SN993), it carries the Yeates Pegasus DP45F body (95362). It is captured on the town service, having come to Lerwick in 1969. It was scrapped in 1975, but as stated, some 25-years on it is still with us today and ripe for preservation. It is ironic when you think of it, the railway preservation scene had the Barry Scrapyard - the bus preservation scene had Shetland, but how many enthusiasts realised it?*

Bottom Left: *In April 1970 a really modern coach was purchased from Healings of Oldham, in the shape of the almost new TBU 823G. This coach featured the new Bedford VAM 70 chassis (9T467101) and the new Duple Viceroy C45F body (1226/174). Interestingly this was one of the last Bedford VAMs to be built with a petrol engine, and the last petrol engined coach purchased by Leask's. The coach, which would last with Leask's until it was scrapped in 1992, is seen here during a tour at Sumburgh carrying passengers from a cruise liner. The driver in the front of the picture is Sidney Hepburn.*

Top Right: *The first brand new coach purchased by Leask's since 1956 came in June 1972, with BPS 987K. This was a Bedford YRQ (2T473303) fitted with a Plaxton Panorama Elite Express C45F body (729667). It is seen here when new, and is just about to leave on tour. The driver, a very young-looking Peter Leask, is seen talking to his father Jamie (seen on the right), just before departure. This coach remained in the Leask fleet until 1997, when it was donated to the Romania Appeal.*

Centre Right Top: *Acquired as a three-year old vehicle in March 1974, this 1971-built Ford R192 (BC04LC54898) was acquired from Barrie of Balloch. XSN 44J had a C45F Plaxton Panorama Elite body (712540), but this was later converted to B45F. Lasting until 1987, when it was scrapped, the Ford is seen here passing Leask's office on the Esplanade. Peter Leask is on the pavement, whilst the driver is Lenny Watt.*

Centre Right Bottom: *Next to join the fleet was HPS 27P, a brand new Bedford YMT (HW452901) which came in June 1976. It had the Plaxton Panorama Supreme Express C53F body (7611TX538), and would remain in the fleet until scrapping in 1993. With Andrew Leask as driver, the coach is on the Overland Service and waiting for the car ferry from Yell at Toft in 1976.*

Bottom Right: *In this colour picture we see HPS 27P in different livery after Leask's added a light blue line in 1983.*

Bottom Left: *Formerly in the Alexander Northern fleet (NAC72), CWG 481 was an AEC Monocoach (MC3RV1184) dating from 1955. This Alexander-bodied B45F (4716) was some 20-years old when it came to Lerwick in 1975. For a relatively short period it was employed on the Town Service, but it did not last very long and was scrapped in 1976. Advertising on bus sides in Shetland was also something of a novelty, and the Pearl Assurance company would have been glad of the exposure for as long as it lasted.*

Top Left: *Another AEC purchased for the Town Service work, was this Reliance (MU3RV1184) dating from 1956. It also came from Alexander Northern (fleet number NAC84), and arrived in Lerwick in October 1975. Registered HMS 233, the AEC again had Alexander B45F bodywork (4943). The styling was somewhat different from GWG 481, but it was very useful for the run around Lerwick. On this work it eked out its days, before being scrapped in 1979 at the age of 23-years.*

Centre Left: *Purchased from Chapman of Airdrie in April 1977, MGG 396P was a 1976 Bedford YRQ (EW450261). It had a Duple Dominant 45-seat body (516/2203) and was fitted with the two-leaf 'express' doors. The driver on this occasion is my younger brother, Victor Jamieson, who was helping out on the liner cruise work. Standing on the pavement outside is another regular Leask driver, Robbie Leask.*

Below: *A further view MGG 396P, this time sporting a new livery.*

This Page: *As mentioned under the Shalder fleet, the changes that took place within any one given operation over a period of years were quite numerous. Not least of all did this prove to be the case in the matter of livery changes, and here I have used three photographs of the same vehicle to show how this change alone could dramatically alter the appearance of a bus or coach. Here we have UHS 602R, Bedford YMT (GW450717) with a Plaxton Supreme C53F body (7711TC171) shown in three different liveries. It came from its original operators Don of Bishop Stortford in March 1978, and as it was only a year old, the livery of that company was retained. As it was not hugely different from the basic Leask colours of blue and cream, this probably did not matter too much. The driver pictured with it in this colour scheme is Tammie Tulloch who drove for Leask's for many years. The subsequent pictures show the livery changes applied to the coach before it was scrapped in 1995.*

Left: *Another example of a coach being operated in the livery of its former owner is seen in the case of KFU 867P, a Bedford NJM (EW456732) with a Plaxton Supreme C41F body (76NJM006). This coach dated from 1976 and was purchased from Hornsby of Scunthorpe in September 1978. It was operated for a while in the Hornsby livery but later repainted in Leask's dark blue and cream.*

Right: *Here we see KFU 867P after it was re-painted into the Leask livery. The coach is awaiting tourists from a visiting cruise ship and its driver is Robbie Leask. The coach stayed in Lerwick until December 1981 when it was traded-in against OPS 742X. This coach was later sold by the dealer (Paul Sykes) to Martindale's of Shildon in the summer of 1982.*

Left: *Purchased new in April 1979, KPS 959T was a Bedford YMT (HW456105) with a Plaxton Supreme IV C53F body (7911TC069). The coach is seen here with Lollie Leask driving on a private charter. At the age of 12-years KPS 959T was traded-in to the dealers Yeates of Loughborough against E700 YNS a Dennis Javelin 8.5SDL.*

Right: *A second view of KPS 959T, but shown wearing the new Leask livery.*

Left: *For work in busy cities the dual entrance bus was found to be ideal as it allowed front entry and centre exit to speed operations. However this was something of an overkill on the Town Service for which Leask's purchased GRS 11E. This was a Leyland (PSUC/13750669). It had an Alexander Y-type B43D body built in 1967 and was originally supplied to Grampian (fleet number RT11). It came to Lerwick in April 1979 and was sold to Johnson Bros., Brae in 1982.*

Right: *In October 1980 the company purchased NPS 161W a brand new Leyland Leopard (PSU3F/5R/7903131). This had a Plaxton Supreme IV Express C53 body (8011LX536) which is seen here at the opening of Sullom Voe oil terminal by the Queen in 1981. The driver is Lollie Leask, one of the sons of the founder John Leask, who later became a partner in the business.*

Centre Left: *Here we see NPS 161W once again, but this time in its second livery whilst it is being driven off Victoria Pier, Lerwick, by Erik Young.*

Centre Right: *A further view of the same coach, now in its third livery, this time the driver is Robbie Leask.*

Below: *Another new Leyland Leopard (PSU3F/5R/8030928) was purchased in December 1981, this time with a Duple Dominant IV C53F body (233/5187). Whilst it is also shown in its second livery on page 112 it is pictured here with Lollie Leask when new.*

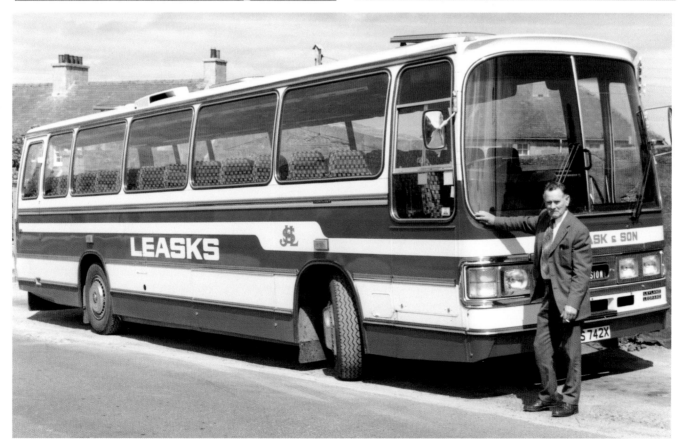

Top Left: *As described overleaf OPS 742X was brand new in 1981. Driven here by Zander Irvine at the Knab in Lerwick, opposite Leask's bus park, this 53-seat coach lasted until June 1992 when it was traded-in against J662 FPS. The dealers (Hughes) sold the vehicle on to A.S.C. of Leeds.*

Centre Left Top: *Another Alexander Y-Type bus was acquired for the town service in 1982, and had 38 dual purpose seats. It had an Albion Viking chassis (VK49L50850A) chassis dating from 1970. Registered ORS 84H it had previously been in service with Alexander Northern (NNV84), and it remained with Leask's until it was scrapped in 1985.*

Centre Left Bottom: *Towards the end of 1983 Leask's acquired the business of A.J. Eunson of Virkie and a number of vehicles from this fleet were absorbed into the Lerwick operation. One of these was MPS 901W a Bedford YMQ (KW452859) with a Plaxton Supreme IV C45F body (8010QX5095). New in August 1980 this coach was repainted into the Leask livery and stayed in the fleet until it was scrapped in 1999.*

Bottom Left: *Also acquired from Eunson in November 1983, PGM 639H was a 13-year old Bedford VAM70 (OT477568). In this picture it still retains the Eunson livery applied to its Duple Viceroy C45 body (211/31). It did no active service with Leask's and was scrapped in 1984.*

Bottom Right: *Another short lived transfer from Eunson's, JAR 614G was a 1969-built AEC Reliance 691 (RE6U3ZR7267). It had a Plaxton Panorama Elite 53-seat body (692929) which was scrapped in 1984.*

Opposite Page Top Left: *A more durable acquisition from Eunson, JPT 774N would last with Leask & Son until 1990 when it was scrapped. This was a Bedford YRQ (EW450672) with a Duple Dominant body (515/2005). It was later converted to bus seating specification, becoming B45F.*

Opposite Page Top Right: *The final vehicle to be absorbed from the Eunson fleet was VYH 499M, another Bedford YRQ (CW451947). It had the Plaxton Elite II C45F body (7410QC011) and it lasted in the Leask fleet until 1990 when it was sold to Shalder Coaches of Scalloway who broke it up for spares.*

Centre Right: *In April 1985 Leask's ordered a new type of chassis, a DAF SB2300DHS (585-243895). Fitted with a Plaxton Paramount 3200 C53F body (8512DRP2C002), this coach (B885 TPS) was retained in the fleet until June 1997 when it was traded-in for H540 YCX. It was later to be seen working for Bibby of Ingleton in North Yorkshire.*

Below: *Another new chassis type was found on A801 TGG, a 1983 MAN MT8.136 (0011182), with a Reeve Burgess Riviera C28F body (14597). Seen at Brekon, Cullivoe, on the island of Yell, this coach was purchased from Stirling of Kilsyth in July 1985. The coach was sold to the Caetano dealers as part of a trade-in on K330 CCC in April 1994. By May it had travelled down to Smiths of Bristol.*

Left: *Although Bristol service buses were common in many parts of Britain, Shetland was not one of them. This RELL6L (3/1569) had an ECW DP50F body (19369). Dating from 1972, EBL 390K arrived in Lerwick in September 1985 from Barwick of Barlow. It was purchased for the Town Service but only lasted until 1986 when it was scrapped.*

Right: *At the age of just 9-months, D353 XPS was purchased from Bolts Coaches. It was new in November 1986 and joined Leask's in September 1987 and lasted with them until March 1997 when it was sold to Carolan, Nobber in Southern Ireland just prior to the arrival of P20 JLS. This 20-seat coach was a Fiat (79F1450078), with a Caetano Viana body (185061).*

Left: *Another local acquisition was NSA 255P, a Ford R1114 (BCO4RJ52279) which came from Grantfield Garage in 1988. It featured a Plaxton Supreme DP58F body (7611FX509) and dated from 1976. It lasted in the Leask fleet until July 1989 when it was sold to a C. Whitney on Yell who intended to convert it to a horsebox. However, this conversion never took place and the Ford was sold to mainland Britain some time afterwards.*

Right: *In 1988 yet another Alexander Y-Type DP50F bus (444Y/2072/8) was purchased to work on a Sullom Voe contract. Coming from Northern Scottish (NBE124) this was registered RAG 390M and was built on a Leyland Leopard chassis (PSU3/327303206). It is seen here in Lerwick, on an occasion when the driver was Peter Leask.*

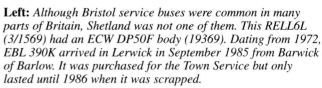

Left: *At the end of its service life the Leyland was withdrawn in September 1993 and donated to the Albanian Appeal. The cream paintwork was covered over in sky blue and the windows blocked out ahead of the long journey to Eastern Europe.*

Right: *Purchased brand new in April 1988, E658 YPS was a DAF SB2300 (DHTD585299214) with a Plaxton Paramount C57 body (8812DMP3C009). It is seen here coming off the ferry* Geira *at Belmont, whilst heading on to Unst with a tour. The driver is once again Robbie Leask.*

Left: *This Fiat IVECO 35-9 (427791) with an Elme C16F body (024/010) dated from October 1986. Leask's purchased it from Arthur of Coatbridge in September 1988 and scrapped it in 1992.*

Right: *Here we have Leask's new acquisition for the summer of 1989. In April of that year they took delivery of a DAF SB2305 DHT585 (318953) and had it fitted with a Plaxton Paramount 3200 C57F body (8912DFA1408) which is seen in the coach-builder's showroom at Scarborough.*

Left: *Seen on the journey back to Shetland from the Plaxton factory in Scarborough Peter (left) and Lollie (right) proudly stand in front of F851 APS*

Right: *When John Leask & Son began their Town Service, critics said that it would not last more than a few months. It is still going today and proves very useful to the people of Lerwick. Over the years a variety of second hand service buses were purchased for this route, but in March 1990 the firm got its first new bus for the town run. This was G621 GPS, a Dennis Javelin (11SDL1914/443) with a Duple B55F body (8824/1014). It stayed in the fleet until 1999 when it was sold to Green Triangle Buses.*

Top *Left:* *In November 1990 Leask's acquired C629 PAU a DAF MB230DKFL (615274536). Coming from Collinson of Stonehouse this May 1986 coach had a Plaxton Paramount 3200 C53F body (8612DVP2C003).*

Centre Left Top: *Here we see E700 YNS, a 35-seat Plaxton Paramount (888DJP3C002) that was purchased from Haldane of Glasgow in May 1991. This had a Dennis Javelin 8.5SDL chassis (1903/150) and dated from February 1988. When it reached 10-years of age it was sold to Eagles & Crawford in North Wales.*

Centre Left Bottom: *New in April 1992, J662 FPS was a DAF SB2305 DHS585 (329804) with a Plaxton Paramount 3200 C55 body (9112DDA2260). Note the low driver position.*

Bottom Left: *In October of 1992 Leask's purchased their first Ford Transit (BDVVMD59579) mini-bus. It had a Dormobile 16-seat body, and offered considerable headroom for the passengers.*

Opposite Page Top: *Here we show G953 KJX with driver Robbie Pottinger in a DAF SB2305 DHTD585 (318913) carrying a Plaxton Paramount (3200) fitted with 57-seats (9012DFA2082). Carrying a Calderdale registration plate this vehicle was obtained from Browne of East Grinstead, and has just been sold to Garry Johnson (Brae) at the time of going to press.*

Opposite Page Bottom: *A line up of five Plaxton Paramount coaches from the Leask fleet, with Peter and Andrew Leask at the front.*

Left: *When John Watt decided to cease his coaching operation his fleet was broken up and sold to various operators. However, one of his coaches KPS 701T had already been sold to John Leask & Son in 1991. This was a Bedford YLQ (JW451717) with a Plaxton Supreme C45F body (7910QX503). Dating from January 1979 the coach joined Leask's fleet in August 1991 and was sold to Shalder Coaches in August 1993. The former owner of James Watt & Son, John Watt, joined Leask's as a driver and he is still with the company at the time of writing.*

Right: *In June 1993 J478 XHL, a 1991 Mercedes 709D (669303-2P-154962) was acquired from Bon Accord Windows in Aberdeen. It was put into PSV use with a Plaxton C25F body (917MCV0539). It was sold to a dealer in Newbridge in November 1998, when it was traded-in against S20 JLS. Later that month the coach was sold to Patterson's of Seahouses in Northumberland.*

Left: *Purchased from K-Line of Kirkburton, Huddersfield in November 1993, YOT 545V was a 1980 Leyland National (NL116L11/2R06861) with a B44D body. It was purchased for work on the town service and sold to Trevor Wigley of Carlton in December 1996 for scrap.*

Right: *Fitted with a toilet, K300 CCC was a MAN 11-190 (WMA4691239G081716) with a Caetano C33F body (TWOA159P259008226). It was new to Cunningham of Corringham in March 1993 and sold to Leask's in April the following year.*

Left: *Purchased new in August 1994 this Renault mini-bus (MTR1648471), with a Jubilee 14-seat conversion M431 HOX provided a useful small capacity vehicle of the Leask fleet.*

Right: *New in April 1995, M20 JLS was a DAF MB230LT (615003651). It had a Van Hool C57F body (31902) and was the first of Leask's vehicles to be given a personalised registration plate.*

Left: *Here we see N746 LUS, which joined the fleet in November 1995. This LDV 400 (CN862039) had an odd B16F body; the production of which was started by Pearl Coaches, but this firm went into liquidation during the build, and the work was later finished by Carlyle.*

Right: *Purchased in May 1996, with their second personalised registration plate (N20 JLS), came DAF DE33WSSB3000 (004840). It was the first coach in the fleet to have the Ikarus body (350TIPSIGB0008). The C55F coach is seen here with Andrew Leask at the wheel whilst passing through Seafield, Lerwick.*

Left: *Another personalised plate, P20 JLS was applied to this Mercedes 711D (WDB6690032NO47450). It had a Plaxton Beaver II C25 body (997/MKY6052) and was supplied to the company in March 1997.*

Right: *Registered in Huddersfield, H540 YCX probably started life through the dealers Hughes of Cleckheaton. It came to Leask's as a six-year old coach in May 1997 from Southern of Barrhead. It was a DAF (SB2305DHS585) with a Plaxton Paramount 3200 C55F body (9112DDA2259). The DAF is seen here waiting to pick up passengers from one of the large cruise liners that visit Lerwick during the summer season.*

Above: *In April 1998 the fourth personalised registration plate was acquired in the form of R20 JLS, as Leask's continued the purchase of DAF chassis. This time they chose the rather stylish Ikarus 350 body with 53-seats (TRA350T1PWIGB0099) for the new DAF (XMGDE33WSOH006253).*

Centre Left: *In 1998 the '20 JLS' plates were continued with S20 JLS, a Mercedes 0814D (WDB6703742N078820). This had a Plaxton Beaver II 31-seat body to Diptac specification (98.8.5MXV9861).*

Bottom Left: *Obtained for a six month loan period from the commercial dealer Arriva, M833 RCP was a 1995 DAF SB 220 LT5S0 (003979). It had the Ikarus 480 B48F body (TRA480V1ARIGB0016). This bus was returned to Arriva in June 1999 but it filled the gap until a batch of four similar vehicles were delivered that same month.*

Opposite Page: *This montage of pictures show the Leask acquisitions of June 1999, with a batch of vehicles registered T20 JLS, T30 JLS, T40 JLS and T50 JLS. These were all DAF DEO2GS SB220 chassis and had the serial numbers H006849 for T20JLS and H007110-2 for T30-40-50 JLS respectively. The body numbers ran consecutively from TRA481VIPWIGB0120-23. In the upper picture T30 and T40 are seen side by side in the Viking Bus Station. The four lower pictures show T20 to T50 in consecutive order.*

GANSON BROTHERS

Based initially at Harbour Street (later moving to Market Street), Ganson Bros. was a long established Lerwick firm who entered the passenger carrying business at an early stage, and remained in it until they sold out to John Leask & Son in 1963. They were haulage contractors who held the contract for the Royal Mail services until these were taken over by the GPO in 1947, and they were also the local Ford agents. In the 1930s they ran an impressive list of services from Lerwick to Sumburgh (via Sandwick and Virkie), North Roe (via Voe, Brae, Sullom and Ollaberry), Sandness (via Walls), Mossbank and Scalloway. They had the contract for Highland Airways to carry passengers to and from the airport, and they also did excursion tours as well. A number of small capacity buses were operated in the 1920s, including PS 159 an Arrol Johnson, an Albion truck that converted to a charabanc, and a series of Model T Fords; these included PS 770 and PS 858.

Above: *Here we see PS 770, the first member of the Ganson fleet that I can positively identify as being a bus with 13 or more seats. It is a 1928 Ford B13F and has a body built in Lerwick by A. Peterson, a local coach-builder. From the crowds seen here, it is obvious that this event was an occasion of note; in fact the picture was taken on the occasion of the first scheduled airplane service to Shetland, with which the Ganson bus would provide a link from Sumburgh to Lerwick.*

Left: *Here we see a pair of the company's later vehicles PS 2001 and PS 2038 at the pier in Lerwick, in a very attractive scene with the* Tjaldur *(a Faroese boat) in the background. The Ganson colours were dark blue and turquoise until 1947, after which they were changed to grey and cream with a red flash to indicate that they carried the Royal Mail.*

The Ganson fleet was:-

Reg.	Chassis	Body	Cap.	Year	Acq.
PS 770	Ford TT	Peterson	B14F	1928	New
YH 7588	Thornycroft	NCME	B20F	1924	1933
RS 8921	Dennis	?	B14F	1925	1933
UP 6358	Ford 24HP	?	B20F	1931	1934
EJ 3157	Ford 24HP	?	B20F	1932	1934
VO 3870	Ford 24HP	?	B14F	1930	1935
WP 345	Ford 24HP	Sunshine	C20F	1933	1935
LG 7198	Bedford WLB	Jennings?	B20F	1933	1936
JI 6007	Fordson 24HP	?	B20F	1934	1938
FKR 607	Fordson 24HP	Appleyard?	C20F	1938	1940
JB 9189	Fordson 24HP	Appleyard?	C20F	1938	1940
EC 8770	Fordson 24HP	?	C20F	1938	1942
RG 2267	Bedford WLB	Duple?	C20F	1931	1943
EFS 183	Bedford OWB	SMT	B28F	1945	1949
EFS 196	Bedford OWB	SMT	B28F	1945	1949
FAO 822	Bedford OWB	SMT	B28F	1945	1949
LWB 756	Guy Vixen	Barnard	C27F	1948	1949
PS 2001	Fordson Thames	Scottish Av	C29F	1950	New
PS 2038	Fordson Thames	Bellhouse	C29F	1950/1	New
SS 7237	Bedford OB	Duple	C29F	1949	1954
FFS 902	Bedford OB	Duple	C29F	1947	1956
KGB 66	Bedford SB	Duple	C33F	1952	1957
KGB 759	Bedford SB	Duple	C33F	1952	1959

Top Right: *Details of the early Ganson fleet are very sketchy and there is conflicting information on the seating capacity of the early vehicles. However, it was not uncommon in the 1920s and 1930s to operate vehicles that had a dual-purpose capability. Commercial vehicles, such as lorries and vans could be given an 'add-on' bus body, or small buses could be made so that their seats were easily removed in order to convert the bus into a delivery van. The second bus we can positively identify as having had 13+ seats was YH 7588. This was a Thornycroft bus with 20-seats, dating from 1924. It was purchased from the North Eastern Railway by W. Alexander & Son in September 1930, and went to work in the Falkirk area until April 1932. It was then sold to the Stirling firm of Kinross & Son, before coming to Shetland the following year.*

Centre Right Top: *A small 6-seat GMC bus, which could convert to a delivery van (RS 2313) was purchased next, along with RS 8921 a 1925 Dennis. This seems to have taken place in June 1933, when the B20F Dennis would have been about eight-years old. It even had the luxury of a destination blind headbox, and from this we can see RS 8921 is pictured on a run to Lerwick.*

Centre Right Bottom: *At rest with its crew, we see a side view of the Northern Counties-bodied RS 8921. We have few other details about this Dennis, including the disposal date. However, as Ganson's were motor mechanics, it is quite possible that the bus may have simply gone into their garage and been dismantled. Alternatively, it was not uncommon for a body to be removed from a bus, and the chassis then turned into a flat bed lorry for use on a croft or farm. In such cases the vehicle would never be registered for road use, and in the case of RS 8921 it simply disappeared from the official record.*

Bottom Right: *Being Ford agents, it was not surprising that a fair percentage of the Ganson's early fleet were of this make. Originating in the Sunderland area UP 6358 was a 24-hp Ford (4792894) from 1931, which later worked in the coal mining district around Langley, County Durham. It came to Lerwick in 1934 from Brewin & Hudson of Heanor in 1934 and lasted for seven years before being scrapped in 1941.*

Above: *In the glorious period picture shown above, we have a 1930s view of the next members of the Ganson fleet, namely a pair of 24-horse power Fords registered EJ 3157 and VO 3870. Of these VO 3870 (AA3018483) was new to the Heanor firm of Brewin & Hudson in 1930, but (like UP 6358) there is a suggestion that this went via Midland General Omnibus of Langley Mill before coming to Lerwick in 1935. It lasted with Ganson until 1943 when it was scrapped. EJ 3157 arrived in the fleet as a two-year old vehicle in 1934, but we have few other details about this 24hp Ford.*

Centre Left: *A second view of EJ 3157 showing the Ganson name on the side.*

Bottom Left: *Also purchased in 1935 was WP 345, another 24hp Ford on which we have very little detail. Like the other acquisitions of this time, it was probably bought to meet the new Royal Mail and passenger contracts. The driver in this picture is called Leask. But when it comes to the next member of the Ganson fleet, LG 7198, this is where I admit to being really stuck, as this bus has proved to be the most illusive vehicle discussed in this book. Despite appealing for information on it for several years, no picture has ever come to light. For a long time I was led to believe that this Bedford WHB (purchased from North Holt, Taunton) had a body made by either Duple or Waveney (see inset advert). However, at the time of going to press some new information suggested that this might have been a Fordson AA (4486688) with an unknown C20F body which was new to J. H. Jennings Ltd. of Sandbach! However, as this was a firm of coachbuilders who were building buses on both Ford and Bedford chassis at the time, it seems likely that this was in fact a Jennings-bodied vehicle. Was it a demonstrator - perhaps you know*

124

Above: *It is so frustrating when information (like that for LG 7198) is missing, especially when such excellent pictures of other members of the fleet have been uncovered. Probably the best picture of the early Ganson fleet is this view of JI 6007, which was taken on the occasion of the last hand-over of mail in 1947. Ganson's had held the contract to carry mail since the mid-1930s, and their buses even had a red stripe painted down the side to signify that they carried 'The Royal Mails', but all this ended in 1947 when the GPO decided to put on their own vans instead. Here we see the formal hand-over, with driver Harry Murray holding the last mail sack. The bus was a 24-hp Fordson, with a B20F body purchased in 1938 as a four-year old vehicle from the Northern Ireland Transport Board. It was obviously still in good working order in 1947, but quite what happened to it I do not know.*

Centre Right: *Conversely I do know what happened to FKR 607, for the body of this bus was converted into a small shop and tea room at Cumleiwick Beach at Sandwick by Frank Matthews, when its working days were over. This body may well have been produced by Appleyard of Leeds, and it was obtained in 1940 as a two-year old vehicle. Once again disposal dates are unclear, and I have no record of when the Fordson actually ended its days as a PSV.*

Bottom Right: *Next in the fleet was JB 9189 another 24-hp Ford from 1938, which came to Lerwick in 1940. Close examination will reveal that it had the same body as the FKR 607, except this was a forward control version, giving a full-front coach. As a result of this arrangement, the drivers called it the 'Rocking Horse' because its suspension gave a very lively ride. This is the only photograph that I have managed to find of JB 9189, but it obviously records an enjoyable day out for the three young ladies pictured in front.*

In 1942 Ganson's purchased a Fordson 24-hp C20F coach registered EC 8770, which dated from 1938. This is another area where I have to admit to complete failure in tracing a photograph showing this vehicle.

Top Left: *During World War II Ganson's purchased RG 2267 from their Lerwick neighbour John Leask & Son. This was a Bedford WLB with an unrecorded C20F body. Shortly after purchase it was requisitioned by the Royal Air Force, who in turn managed to drive it into a roadblock. As it suffered a lot of damage in this incident it was parked up at the Ganson garage, only to suffer further storm damage before it was eventually sold to W. Thomson of Sandwick in 1945.*

Centre Left Top: *In 1949, with vehicles in short supply, they were forced to obtain whatever was available to modernise the fleet. As a result three Bedford OWBs were purchased, two directly from SMT. The first of these was EFS 183 (chassis number 23908), which had a SMT B28F body. Formerly fleet number C128, it is seen here on the North Roe and Hillswick service. It was sold to A. K. Anderson of Mid Yell in 1956.*

Centre Left Bottom: *From the same SMT fleet (fleet number C141) Ganson's obtained EFS 196 (chassis number 24840). This bus lasted until 1957 when it was sold to J.C. Jamieson of Cullivoe for use as a mobile grocery and butchers van.*

Bottom Left: *The third and final OWB was yet another SMT-bodied B28F, which was built in 1945 and came to Lerwick in 1949. Few other details have emerged on this Carlisle-registered bus, which was sold to Irvine Bros. of Boddam in 1954. Registered FAO 822 it is seen here at Bigton.*

Bottom Right: *Another 1949 acquisition was LWB 756 a Guy Vixen (41327) with a Barnard C27F body. It was just one year old when purchased in 1949, but it only lasted until 1956 when it was scrapped. The driver seen here is Harry Murray.*

Opposite Page: *In 1950 Ganson's ordered a new bus on the Fordson Thames ET6 chassis (7235576), which would be registered PS 2001. It had its truck chassis extended by about three feet to make it suitable for a PSV body. When new it was fitted with an 8-cylinder petrol engine, but after some years Ganson Bros. changed this for a 4-cylinder petrol engine which resulted in much lighter fuel consumption. The Scottish Aviation body was constructed mostly from aluminium using surplus war-time aircraft parts. All the panels were held on by self tapping screws, rather than being screwed to wooden covered steel beams, so the body was almost indestructible. The only steel parts left on the body were the Fordson bonnet and the front mud wings. Ganson's had also ordered another ET6 chassis (7244034) to be fitted with an identical body, but as PS 2001 was so expensive to build, they changed the second body (for PS 2038) to one made by Bellhouse Hartwell. In 1964 PS 2001 was sold to our family firm and the following year PS 2038 was withdrawn, but as we go to press this still remains in Shetland as a derelict hulk.*

Above: *The penultimate purchase by Ganson's is shown out of sequence due to it being a period colour picture. The coach, KGB 66, was a Bedford SB (1781) and was fitted with a Plaxton Venturer C33F body. New in 1952 the coach was purchased in 1957 from Row of Muirkirk and sold to a contractor named Tawse when the business finished in 1964.*

Centre Left: *Purchased in 1954, SS 7237 was a Bedford OB (109966), with a Duple Vista C29F body (54296) from 1949. It was purchased from Stark of Dunbar in 1954 and sold to J. J. & A. Leslie in 1959.*

Bottom Left: *FFS 902 was a second Bedford OB (47961) with the Duple Vista body (52510), and had been built in May 1947. It was purchased in April 1956 from Alexander's where it had been fleet number W197. In 1963 it was sold to Garriock of Wester Skeld for spare parts.*

Bottom Right: *The last purchase was KGB 759 a Bedford SB (1094) with a Brush body which came from Whiteford of Lanark as a seven-year old vehicle in 1959. It went to Leask's with the business in 1964.*

In Lerwick, there have been a number of small operators over the years. As will be appreciated in this commercial centre of Shetland a number of ventures have been started in public transport, some have been successful, others have not. Some never reached the 13+ seat capacity vehicles, whilst others only had a single vehicle. These are the ones that I have discovered.

T.L. SINCLAIR

Very little is known about the firm of Thomas L. Sinclair of Lerwick, but it was a very important pioneer and probably started alongside a haulage and hire car operation. In the years between the two world wars, they began a service from Lerwick out to Walls, and it was on this run that Peter Isbister started as a driver. The firm started out with Arrol-Johnston and Model T Ford saloons, and these carried very early Shetland plates like PS 267, PS 269, PS 344 and PS 392. The history of this fleet is a very grey area, but as they were all under 13-seats, it is of only passing interest within the scope of this book.

The first 'big' bus to be operated was a Bedford WHB (100103), registered FS 5896. This dated from 1933 and was fitted with a Duple B14F body. It was purchased from Thomson of Sandwick in 1948 having previously been owned by Ewart's of Haddington. Sadly no picture of this vehicle has survived, and in its stead we have (top right) a similar Bedford/Duple in Lerwick as a representation of the type of scene that could have been witnessed in the late-1940s. This view shows another Bedford-Duple, P.J. Smith's long wheel-based WH registered AV 9364.

TAIT OF LERWICK

The next operator to consider in Lerwick was R. W. Tait of 4, Market Street, who owned RG 2186 and a Peterson-bodied Chevrolet of 10 to 12 seats. RG 2186 was a Commer Invader with a Walker C20F body (pictured centre right top), which is seen whilst in the ownership of R. W. Tait. This picture was loaned to me by a relation of the family, but the event and location is unrecorded. So, if you recognise anyone in this picture, I'd be delighted to know!

GRANTFIELD GARAGE

This was a very short-lived operation, lasting little more than a couple of years. Grantfield Garage is a long-established business based in Lerwick, who obtained a contract to carry workers to the Sullom Voe oil terminal in 1984. To undertake this work they purchased NSA 255P, a 1976 Ford R1114 (BCO4RJ52279) with a Plaxton Supreme DP58F body (7611FX509). At the end of the contract it was sold to Leask's who retained the vehicle in the fleet until July 1989. As seen in the picture centre right bottom, the livery of Grantfield was red and white.

UPSTAIRS-DOWNSTAIRS SHOP

Double-deck buses in Shetland are very rare beasts indeed, and apart from the Bristol Lodekka with an ECW body, which Shalder operated for a short time, no other double-deck service buses have been used in the islands. However, that does not mean that no other double-deckers were to be seen in Shetland, for as this picture shows, there was at least one other. This was a Daimler Fleetline with an Alexander double-deck body, registered CWG 915L which came to Lerwick in the colours of Alexander Northern.

It was purchased with the novel idea of being used as a travelling shop, and was given the prosaic name 'Upstairs Downstairs.' However the venture was not a great success, and after a few short runs the 1972-built bus was parked up. I think it was eventually scrapped as the cost of shipping it back to Aberdeen would have been too costly. However, I did not keep a detailed record of this vehicle, as it was not used for its constructed purpose whilst it was in Shetland. Nevertheless as a photographic record exists, it makes an interesting inclusion in the book!

SHETLAND ISLANDS COUNCIL

Whilst many local authorities entered the field of municipal bus operation back in the 19th-Century, it was the town of Huddersfield who were the first to offer a publicly-owned undertaking from 1868 onwards. Huddersfield Corporation Transport Department may have been the first to offer tram or bus service, but hundreds of other towns followed suit all over Britain; yet in many areas the provision of public services was left to private operators - as was the case in Shetland. By the mid-1930s a national picture had emerged that certain sectors of society were not being catered for, and the first such group to be identified were 'sickly or disabled' schoolchildren.

With the coming of new social responsibilities under the Nation Health Act (1946), those local authorities in Britain who had no public transport facilities, found they were obligated to provide them. As this obligation centred on sick, elderly, infirm or disabled passengers, some councils used ambulances to transport passengers to day centres, special schools, and even on trips and outings. Naturally this was found to be a wasteful use of an emergency ambulance, and buses were obtained instead. In some areas this change did not take place until local government re-organisation in 1973-4, but as the needs of 'disadvantaged' groups became assessed, the Shetland Islands Council developed a fleet of vehicles to meet the special needs.

Above: *Here we see LSC 62, a Bristol LS6B(101155), which had an Eastern Counties C38F body (7770) with cant rail windows. This was the first bus purchase by the SIC to be used for the transport of elderly and disabled passengers.*

Centre Left: *Next we see EMS 966S a Leyland FG with a Maclay body, which came new in 1978.*

Bottom Left: *New in 1981, the SIC introduced NPS 256W Bedford YRQ (KW453684) with a modified Duple Dominant body (116/2250), which provided 28 fitted seats. It was sold to Bolts Coaches who took the work on contract in 1988.*

Reg.	Chassis	Body	Cap.	Year	Acq.
LSC 62	Bristol	ECW	C38	1954	1975
EMS 966S	Leyland FG	Maclay	?	1978	1981
NPS 256W	Bedford YRQ	Duple	C28	1981	1981
A298 SPS	Bedford VAS 5	Plaxton	C25	1983	1983
E278 YPS	Volvo B10M-46	Plaxton	C26	1987	1987
H277 DPS	Dennis Javelin	Duple	C31	1990	1990

Please note the door arrangement has not been quoted for these vehicles, as they were all modified to provide disabled access.

Top Right: *The next new bus to be obtained by the SIC was A298 SPS, this was a Bedford VAS5 (DT106845) with a modified Plaxton Supreme body (838PJS4C09A). It arrived in Lerwick in October 1983 and had fixed seating for 25 passengers, along with wheelchair spaces. It left the island in October 1991 when it went to the Loughborough dealers, Yeates, who later sold it to Perry of Blackwood.*

Centre Right: *The SIC fleet was expanded in October 1987 by the acquisition of E278 YPS. This was a Volvo B10M-46 (11566) with a Plaxton Paramount body modified to provide 26-seats (8795VMP3C01A). It was sold in July 1997 to Dereham Coaches of East Dereham in Norfolk. Like H277 DPS that followed, this bus was contracted to an operator who ran it on behalf of the SIC. This contract was first given to Bolts Coaches, then Shalder but Leask's operated it the longest until it ended in 1997.*

Below: *This Dennis Javelin (8.5SDA1915/409) came to Lerwick in September 1990. It had a modified Duple body that provided 31 fixed seats, and had the body number 8880/0956. It also lasted until July 1997 when it was sold to the same operator as E278 YPS.*

The long tapering tale of Shetland runs down from Lerwick to Sumburgh Head, and has a very long history including Iron Age, Norse and Dutch settlements. In more recent times the South Mainland provided the island with its main airport, which is located at Sumburgh.

W. THOMSON

One of the operators based in the South Mainland was William Thomson of Swinister, Sandwick who was initially involved in car-hire operation. He also began a goods service and developed into passenger carrying work, after he purchased a Model T Ford in or around 1923. A six-seat Flying Standard was also purchased during the 1920s. In 1936 he purchased their first big bus a 1930 Chevrolet. During 1940 he purchased the garage of Charlie Thomson in Lerwick, and went on to become the Vauxhall-Bedford main dealer, although he later appointed Algar Sutherland to manage this enterprise. In 1959 William Thomson died but the bus business continued to be operated by Mrs Thomson and Magnus Goudie until it was merged with P. J. Smith in 1962 to become the Sandwick Transport Company under the control of Algar Sutherland..

Above: *This is the 1930 Chevrolet, SY 4220, with a C14F SMT body, purchased in 1936. It came from Alexander in Edinburgh and was scrapped in 1941. The next vehicle FS 5896, was the third WTB (100103) built by Bedford, and had a SMT body. Sadly no photograph of this B14F bus has thus far emerged, but a representative picture is seen on page 129. It came to Thomson in 1938 and was sold to T.L. Sinclair ten years later.*

Above: *A very poor photo is all that we have to show ASD 100, a Bedford OWB with a Duple Utility B28F body, purchased in 1945 from Shand, Tarland. It lasted until 1952, when it was sold to Hunter Bros. of Weisdale. It is seen here to the right of the picture in the company of PS 1407 at the opening of the Muckle Roe Bridge in the late-1940s.*

Centre Right: *Although already shown before, RG 2267 has to be included here, as this is the Bedford WLB coach damaged after a collision with a road block at 'Lang Kames' in the war. Thomson purchased the damaged body around about 1945, and repaired the canvas roof with a fishing boat sail. For years afterwards this coach could be seen with the boat's 'LK' registration letters on its canvas roof.*

Top Left: *Purchased new in April 1946, PS 1407 was a Bedford OB (15088) with a Duple Vista C29F body (42186). It remained with Thomson until April 1953 when it was sold to Georgeson & Moore.*

Top Right: *Obtained from Anderson of Bonchester Bridge in 1950, came this one-year old Bedford OB (117160) Fitted with a Mulliner II B28F body (T500), BKS 179 was sold to the Trustees of T. R. Manson in 1952.*

Centre Right: *Here we see LSM 44, a Duple Vista-bodied (51289) Bedford OB (146975) with driver John Duncan, this coach was acquired in 1954 from Green of Lochmaben in 1954. It was sold to Johnson of Scalloway in 1956 - please note that for reasons of space, this picture is shown out of sequence from the purchase dates.*

Bottom Right: *In 1950 the firm purchased HGE 219 from the Scottish Co-Operative Wholesale Society in Glasgow. This Bedford OB (137703), with a Duple Vista C29F body (56575) was almost brand new. It had been purchased from the SCWS, who had ordered it some time earlier to fulfil a railway-bus link service, but by the time it arrived this contract had been cancelled and it was surplus to requirement. Research at the National Railway Museum in York indicates that this service would have been for the London Midland Scottish Railway in the Loch Lomond area. From what we understand, the coach was to have been painted in the LMS maroon paint scheme, and some little time ago a pair of transfers turned up in Rutherglen with the registration number HGE 219 written on the top. These varnish-slide transfers display the LMS Railway coat of arms and the LMS stock number 43850 - they have subsequently been donated by the owner to the Viking Coach Trust. Why these transfers should carry the 1950 registration number HGE 219 is something of a mystery, as the LMS was absorbed into British Railways on 1st January 1948. Whatever the case HGE 219 passed to Johnson's of Scalloway in 1954 and later went to James Watt & Son of Reawick. This coach finally passed into preservation and it still remains at the start of the 21st Century, in the care of the Paradise Collection owned by John Mould of Reading.*

Reg.	Chassis	Body	Cap.	Year	Acq.
SY 4220	Chevrolet	SMT	C14F	1930	1936
FS 5896	Bedford WHB	SMT	B14F	1933	1938
RG 2267	Bedford WLB	Duple	C20F	1931	1945
ASD 100	Bedford OWB	Duple	B28F	1944	1945
PS 1407	Bedford OB	Duple	C29F	1946	1946
BKS 179	Bedford OB	Mulliner	B28F	1949	1950
HGE 219	Bedford OB	Duple	C29F	1950	1950
ERG 164	Bedford OB	Duple	C29F	1950	1953
LSM 44	Bedford OB	Duple	C29F	1951	1954
PS 2107	Bedford SB	Duple	C33F	1951	1956
BSY 929	Bedford SBG	Duple	C36F	1955	1961

Top Left: *Purchased in 1953 ERG 164 was a Bedford OB (145540), which came from Patterson's of Aberdeen. This 1950-built coach was the only Duple Vista (56575) in Shetland with cant rail windows just below the roof. This little extra actually cost just £30, but only about 4% of the OBs had this feature. Although it may not sound a great deal by today's standards, £30 would now be around £563, so it is not surprising that few coaches buyers avoided this luxury in the austerity years after World War II. The coach itself remained with Thomson's until 1961 when it was sold to the Trustees of T. R. Manson, West Sandwick, Yell.*

Centre Left: *Offering four more seats than the Duple Vista. the new Duple Vega C33F coach was introduced at the end of 1950. This example (56820) was on a Bedford SB chassis (2440) and dated from 1951. Registered PS 2107 it was new to John Leask & Son, who sold it to Thomson in March 1956. It was one of two coaches that would pass to the new Sandwick Transport Company in 1962.*

Below: *A later model Bedford SBG (36211) with a Duple Super Vega C36F body (1055/256) was purchased in 1961 from Allen of Gorebridge. Dating from 1955, BSY 929 was the last bus to be bought by Thomson, and it presents a striking picture in its tan and cream colour scheme when seen in the bus park at Lerwick.*

P. J. SMITH

Based at Hillcrest, Sandwick, this firm first appears in local registration records as W. J. Smith just after World War I. However, it seems as though Smith was in business operating a goods and hackney service before 1914. Services to Lerwick (direct) and via Wester Quarff were operated, but the buses were all 12 seats or under. In 1938 the firm obtained an eight-year old Chevrolet (U65407), which was purchased from Hunter of Loanhead. This in turn was sold to A. Ratter of Ollaberry in 1942. It was replaced by a Bedford WLB, which was well-used but kept on the road until 1947, when a 'new' 14-seat Bedford was acquired. After the war, Smith was succeeded in the business by his son Peter. He continued in the firm until 1961, when J. Smith, the owner of Bolts Garage in Lerwick took an interest in the business. Algar Sutherland was appointed as manager, and he went on to oversee the merger with Thomson's in April 1962. The resulting Sandwick Transport Co. will be discussed later.

Reg.	Chassis	Body	Cap.	Year	Acq.
SC 7513	Chevrolet	?	C14F	1930	1938
AV 9364	Bedford WLB	Duple	C20F	1932	1942
PS 1595	Bedford MW	Home Conv.	B14F	1947	1947
CWV 796	Bedford OWB	Duple	B28F	1944	1949
AMS 339	Bedford OWB	SMT	B28F	1944	1950
CWH 340	Bedford OB	Pearson	C26F	1948	1954
SK 2862	Bedford OWB	Duple	C26F	1944	1954
FRV 740	Austin KCXD	Churchill	C32F	1951	1956

Top Left: *Smith's first big bus, the 14-seat Chevrolet SC 7513.*

Top Right: *Taken from a much larger picture showing Lerwick Harbour, we see bus number two (AV 9364). This was a Bedford WLB with a Duple C20F body, which was probably painted in the company's black and yellow livery.*

Centre Right Top: *Although I have said that PS 1595 was a 'new' bus acquired in 1947, it was anything but; the chassis was a former Bedford MW military truck (MWD33430), and the body was from the ex-MacBrayne Morris Commercial which had stood idle since it was withdrawn by Robert Sandison in 1937. It was converted to fit the square nosed Bedford, which would have made it completely unique. We have no picture of the vehicle with Smith, but this view shows it at Baltasound after being sold to J.G. Hunter on Unst in 1950.*

Centre Right Bottom: *We have no photograph of the Duple-bodied OWB CWV 796, which was supplied new to an operator in the north of England in 1944. This is quite a shame, as Peter Smith modified the entry doors to make them driver-operated. We do have its tax disc for 1956 however.*

Bottom Right: *The bus CWV 796 would however, have looked the same as the next OWB (24683) AMS 339. Although this bus had a body by SMT, there was little difference in the two. It was purchased from J. Peterson, Ollaberry in 1950, and was sold to J. Moncrieff of Spiggie in 1956.*

Above: *The coach-building firm of Pearson's from Liverpool, is not one of the better known names of the 1940s. Yet not only were they body builders, but they also operated their own fleet called Sunnyways Coaches. After the war they re-bodied a large number of OWBs and also built quite a few new OBs as well. One of these was CWH 340 made for the Lancashire firm Enterprise Motors from whom it was purchased in 1954. It had the chassis number 66498, and carried 26 passengers. It may interest readers to know that several hundred photographs, showing the vital work carried on by Pearson's during World War II, have been loaned to Trans-Pennine, and will make the basis of a future book. This coach was one of two that passed to the new Sandwick Transport Co. in 1962.*

Below: *A third Bedford OWB (21535) was purchased in 1954, this time with a Duple C26F body (38881). New to Highland Omnibus (fleet C8) in 1944, SK 2862 was not required by Sandwick Transport for long and was thus sold to J. Moncrieff in 1956.*

Below: *Hardly the most attractive of vehicles, FRV 740 was an Austin KCXD (178187) with a Churchill C32F body.. It dated from 1951, and was purchased as a five-year old coach from Feltham Transport. It passed to Sandwick Transport in 1962. The merger of the two companies was remarked upon in a 1965 issue of the* Buses Illustrated *magazine, which said 'The Sandwick Transport Company, a recent amalgamation of two local businesses demonstrates what can be achieved by sensible rationalisation of competing service.' The magazine went on to highlight that one of the best-used services was the 10.30pm run from Lerwick on Saturday nights, which was well used by passengers returning from the cinema, many of whom were probably courting couples.*

THE SANDWICK TRANSPORT COMPANY

As mentioned earlier, an astute piece of rationalisation came to the Shetland bus scene in 1962, when two long-established firms were merged into one concern. As noted, W. Thomson died in 1959, and his widow continued the business with the aid of Magnus Goudie. In due course both the Lerwick garage and the bus business came under the management of Algar Sutherland. As Peter Smith was also looking to retire around the same time, his business was absorbed with Thomson's, and out of the two fleets, four buses were retained to form Sandwick Transport. These were:

Reg.	Chassis	Body	Cap.	Year	Acq
PS 2107	Bedford SB	Duple	C33F	1951	1962
BSY 929	Bedford SBG	Duple	C36F	1955	1962
CWH 340	Bedford OB	Pearson	C26F	1948	1962
FRV 740	Austin KCXD	Churchill	C32F	1951	1962

In the years that followed, the vehicles listed below were added to the fleet:-

Reg.	Chassis	Body	Cap.	Year	Acq
SS 7376	Bedford OB	Duple	C29F	1949	1963
PS 1805	Austin K2/SL	Federated Ind.	B20F	1949	1968
VYT 630	Bedford SB3	Duple	C41F	1959	1969
KBV 263	Bedford SB3	Duple	C41F	1956	1970
EDC 313D	Bedford VAM 5	Duple	C45F	1966	1974
GPS 155N	Bedford YRQ	Duple	C45F	1975	1975
CWG 482	AEC Monocoach	Alexander	B45F	1955	1975
KET 30F	Bedford VAM14	Plaxton	C45F	1968	1976
MXG 106G	Bedford VAS 5	Duple	C29F	1969	1977
HUG 190N	Bedford YRQ	Plaxton	C45F	1975	1978
KPS 822T	Bedford PJK	Duple	C29F	1978	1978
LPS 210T	Bedford YLQ	Duple	C45F	1979	1979
LPS 963V	Bedford YLQ	Duple	C45F	1979	1979

In March 1981, the Sandwick Transport operation was re-formed into Bolts Coaches, after the acquisition of the Brae-based Johnson Brothers.

Above: *Photographed in the two different colour schemes employed by the Sandwick Transport Company, we see a line up of the company's Duple-bodied Bedfords across the road from the garage in Sandwick. From left to right we have Super Vega (BSY 929), followed by Vista SS 7376, Super Vega II (YVT 630) and Super Vega (KBV 263). Three of the coaches are in the old tan and cream livery, whilst the OB is in the orange and cream that was applied from the 1970s onwards.*

Below: *Undoubtedly a very attractive orange and cream livery was applied to Bedford OB (121153) SS 7376 by the Sandwick Transport Co. around 1977-8. This Duple Vista C29F (54209) was the first bus bought by the new company, and was acquired the year following the merger from McKinlay of Preston Pans. It lasted in the fleet until as late as 1981, at which time it was sold to a museum in Devon for preservation.*

Opposite Page Top and Bottom: *If every picture is worth a thousand words, then here we have at least two thousand words worth of really superb images.*

In the upper picture we have another view of SS 7376, which is of such quality that, although I have already shown this bus overleaf, my publisher insisted that we have a second view of the coach. Quite what date this picture was taken I have no idea, but it captures the 'rustic' quality of the Shetland bus services in the 1970s.

The lower picture shows another coach that went into preservation, this time PS 1805 an Austin K2SL (135527) with a Federated Industries B20F body. New to James Watt & Son in 1949, it was purchased from the Reawick company in 1968. It stayed with Sandwick until 1975 when it went south for preservation with Henley's Transport.

Top Right: *When Sandwick Transport was formed, they continued the tan and cream livery of W. Thomson, and this is seen on the next member of the fleet VYT 630. This was a 1959 Bedford SB3 (66544) with a Duple Super Vega II C41F body (1105/40). It was purchased in 1969 from Netherfield, and was eventually scrapped at Sandwick, but I do not have the date for this.*

Centre Right Top: *In 1970, a 1956 SB3 (59774) with a Duple Super Vega body (1090/299) was purchased from Taylor's London SE1. The 41-seat coach, registered KBV 263, was also scrapped by the company at the end of its working life, but I do not have a date for this. Like the Super Vega II pictured above, this Super Vega had the luxury of the optional roof cant rail windows.*

Centre Right Bottom: *In 1974 Sandwick acquired a more modern Duple-Bodied Bedford, this was EDC 313D dating from 1966. Built on a Bedford VAM5 chassis (6821649), it was fitted with a Duple Bella Venturer C45F body (1205/189). Once again it is one of the few coaches that I have been unable to find disposal details for, but it was acquired from an operator called Sharky of Shott.*

Bottom Right: *After years of purchasing second-hand vehicles, the company got its first new vehicle in the form of GPS 155N in 1975. The time for purchasing new vehicles was ripe, as the grant regime, favourable for several years in the early-1970s, was to be considerably reduced in the years ahead. The marketing departments of several chassis manufacturers (especially Ford, Bedford and British Leyland) each joined forces with body-builders like Duple and Plaxton, and a concerted effort was made to promote sales of new vehicles at the end of 1974. Many orders were duly placed at the annual bus show at the end of the year, and one of those that were processed at the Bedford factory in Dunstable was for a Bedford YRQ (EW450810). The chassis went north to the Duple factory at Blackpool in December 1974, but it was to be some time before it was fitted with a Dominant Express II C45F body (516/2215). The coach arrived with the new livery of orange and cream, and was to pass into the ownership of Bolts Coaches when the firm was re-formed in March 1981.*

Top Left: *In 1975 Sandwick Transport obtained a contract in connection with work at Sullom Voe and to operate it they purchased CWG 482 from Alexander Northern. Having had the fleet number NAC78, this 20-year old 45-seat bus was no spring chicken when it arrived at Sandwick. As may be expected the AEC Monocoach (MC3RV140) with an Alexander body (4721) was not a great success and having no further use for it, Sandwick scrapped the bus a year later.*

Centre Left: *Riley of Rotherham supplied the Sandwick Transport Company with their next vehicle, this time a Bedford VAM14 (7815248) registered KET 30F. It was built in 1968 with a Plaxton Panorama C45F body (672374). It joined the fleet in 1976 and remained at work for five years before it passed to Bolts Coaches in March 1981.*

Below: *Here we show MXG 106G, a 1977 coach purchased from Balgownie, Bridge of Don Aberdeen. This was a Bedford VAS5 (464457) which had a Duple Bella Vista C29F body (1223/13). It was another of the vehicles that would be handed over to the new Bolts Coaches in March 1981.*

Opposite Page Top: *Originally registered in Leeds in 1975, HUG 190N was purchased from Anderton of Keighley, West Yorkshire, in 1978. It had a Bedford YRQ chassis (EW451606) with a Plaxton Panorama Elite C45F body (7510QC029). It was yet another coach that would transfer to Bolts when the business expanded after the acquisition of Johnson Bros., Brae. It is shown here in the livery that it arrived in at Sandwick in 1978.*

Centre Right: *To continue the modernisation of the fleet, KPS 822T was purchased new in 1978. This was a Bedford PJK (HW453800) carrying a Duple Dominant C29F body (912/1070). The PJK chassis continued the role of the Bedford VAS, and provided operators with a good small coach chassis; in many ways it was the legitimate successor of the Bedford OB, but you'd never guess it from the pictures in this chapter. It is of course worth noting that when the PJK arrived, Sandwick still had the 29-seat OB (SS 7376) in their fleet.*

Bottom Left: *Further new purchases were made in 1979, with a pair of Bedford YLQs being ordered with Duple Dominant II 45-seat bodies. The first of these was LPS 210T, it had chassis number JW452395 and body number 915/2143.*

Bottom Right: *Arriving in November LPS 963V had chassis number JW458140 and body number 016/2251. Like all the coaches pictured on this page, it would enter the 'new' Bolts fleet in the spring of 1981.*

BOLTS COACHES

As I have already mentioned, 1961-2 saw the involvement of Algar Sutherland in the Shetland bus business, when he took over the two Sandwick business of Thomson and Smith. By 1981 the Sutherland family had substantially expanded both the bus business and the garage in Lerwick, now called Bolts Garage. By 1983 the small, elderly fleet of 1961 had been substantially improved to about eight relatively modern coaches. With the coming of the oil industry to Shetland, many businesses witnessed a time of expansion, and this was particularly true of the car hire business operated by Bolts. It was only natural that they should also want to expand their bus interests as well, and this began with the acquisition of the Johnson Brothers business at Brae. This gave Bolts three depots; one in Brae, one in Lerwick and one at Sandwick, the vehicles taken over from Sandwick Transport are all pictured on the opposite page, whilst those later purchased by Bolts are listed below:-

Reg.	Chassis	Body	Cap.	Year	Acq.
OPS 465X	Ford	Dormobile	C16F	1982	New
MGE 88Y	Bedford YNT	Plaxton	C53F	1982	New
EGB 792W	Bedford YNT	Duple	C53F	1981	1983
EMA 461K	Seddon Pen.IV	Plaxton	C53F	1972	1983
HAY 777L	Bedford YRQ	Duple	C45F	1973	1983
XWK 17X	Bedford YNT	Plaxton	C53F	1981	1984
HOR 322L	Bedford YRQ	Plaxton	C45F	1972	1984
USE 500R	Bedford YMT	Duple	C53F	1977	1984
A343 SPS	Fiat 60F10	Moseley	C18F	1984	New
A416 SPS	Bedford YNT	Plaxton	C53F	1984	New
A257 ASG	Bedford YMP	Plaxton	C35F	1984	1985
A106 MAC	Bedford YNT	Plaxton	C53F	1984	1985
D353 XPS	Fiat	Caetano	C22F	1986	New
VBM 718W	DAF MB200	Plaxton	C46F	1981	1987

Above: *A line up of Bolts Coaches at Seafield (with Lerwick in the background) featuring, from left to right:- A343 SPS, A416 SPS, XWK 17X, LPS 963V, MGE 88Y.*

Centre Left: *Purchased new in 1982, OPS 465X was a Ford Transit (BDVPAT440170) with a 16-seat Dormobile body (9120). It would pass to Shalder Coaches in 1988.*

Bottom Left: *Also new, in the latter part of 1982 was this Bedford YNT (DT100817). Registered MGE 88Y it featured a Plaxton Paramount 3200 C53F body (8311NTPIC023). It was sold in 1987, and was shipped across to the Orkney islands, where it entered service with the firm of J.D. Peace.*

Above: *EDC 313D, Bedford VAM 5/Duple Bella Venturer.*

Above: *GPS 155N, Bedford YRQ/Duple Dominant C45F.*

Above: *KET 30F, Bedford VAM14/Plaxton Panorama C45F.*

Above: *MXG 106G, Bedford VAS 5/Duple Bella Vista C29F.*

Above: *HUG 190N, Bedford YRQ/Plaxton Panorama Elite.*

Above: *KPS 822T, Bedford PJK/Duple Dominant C29F.*

Above: *LPS 210T, Bedford YLQ/Duple Dominant II C45F.*

Above: *LPS 963V, Bedford YLQ/Duple Dominant C45F.*

Top Left: *This Bedford YMT (KW451981) was a Duple Dominant II C53F (017/2464). Registered EGB 792W, it was new in 1981 and came to Shetland in 1983 from Bywater of Rochdale. It remained with Bolts until 1987, after which it was sold to J.D. Peace in Orkney.*

Top Right: *First registered at Stockport in Cheshire, EMA 461K was an unusual chassis type for Shetland; it was the Seddon Pennine IV (51590). It carried a Plaxton Panorama C53F body (729447) which dated from 1972. It was one of two coaches purchased from A.J. Eunson in 1983.*

Centre Right Top: *The second vehicle to be purchased from Eunson in 1983 was HAY 777L. This was a Bedford YRQ (CW452172) with a Duple Dominant C45F body (266/32). It was 10-years old when it came to Bolts and it lasted with them for five years. In 1988 it was sold to Shalder Coaches of Scalloway, who later scrapped it along with EMA 461K.*

Centre Right Bottom: *The firm of Shaw, Bedworth, supplied the next member of the Bolts fleet, XWK 17X. This was a 1981 Plaxton Supreme V C53F (H21198S5C008) on a Bedford YNT chassis (LW452505). It was purchased in 1984 and sold to Shalder Coaches in 1988.*

Bottom Left: *Another 1984 purchase, HOR 323L, dated from 1972 and was purchased from Sullom Voe Engineering. The coach, which is seen here driven by Billy Bain, was a Bedford YRQ (2T473649) with a Plaxton Panorama Elite III C45F body (728358). It was another of the coaches that would eventually go to Shalder in 1988.*

Top Right: *USE 500R was a Bedford YMT (GW450618) dating from 1977. It was purchased from Arma, Aberdeen, in April 1984 and was sold to Shalder Coaches in 1988. It had a Duple Dominant II C53F body (717/2358).*

Centre Left Top: *Although hardly the most handsome looking coach, A343 SPS provided a useful 18-seat capacity vehicle after it was purchased new in 1984. It was a Fiat 60F10 (350018) with a Moseley Continental body (182160). It also went to Shalder Coaches in 1988.*

Centre Right: *Another new purchase in 1984 was A416 SPS, which would pass into Shalder ownership in 1988. This was a Bedford YNT (DT100792) built at the end of 1983, with a Plaxton Paramount 3200 C53F body (8311NTP1C026).*

Centre Left Bottom: *In 1984 Bedford also produced a YMP (DT105542), which was bodied by Plaxton with a Paramount 3200 C35F body (838MQPIC012). Purchased from Drummond of Harthill in 1985, A257 ASG was sold to James Dunbar of Elgin in April 1988.*

Bottom Right: *A106 MAC was a Bedford YNT (ET103969), which also had the 53-seat Plaxton Paramount 3200 body (8411NTPIC092). Built in 1984 the coach was purchased from Shaw of Bednorth in October 1985 and was sold to Shalder Coaches in 1988. This sale came about after a decision was made to wind down the Bolts Coaches operation, following the reduction in business which came about after the construction work at Sullom Voe ended. Under the management of George Sutherland, the business had gone from strength to strength before it was sold to Shalder Coaches in 1988. Their car hire and self-drive business fleet numbered into the hundreds at its peak, and provided a vital service to the many people who came to Shetland in the oil boom years. Since that time George Sutherland has re-developed his former garage site, and in its place created the attractive Toll Clock Shopping Centre in Lerwick.*

Above: *The last new vehicle to be purchased by Bolts was this 22-seat Iveco Fiat (79F1450078) with a Caetano Viana body (185061). New to the Lerwick operator in November 1986, D353 XPS was purchased by J. Leask & Son in 1987 when Bolts down-sized their fleet.*

Below: *The very last coach to be purchased came from Grangeburn of Motherwell in 1987. Registered VBM 718W, it was a 1981 DAF MB200DKTL600 (196021) with a Plaxton Supreme IV C46F body (8112DC002). It also went to Shalder in 1988.*

J. MONCRIEFF

Operating from Spiggie, J.S. Moncrieff would have a fleet of three buses over the years he operated (1948-1964), but he only ever ran one at a time. He began operating school runs, but later lost this contract and applied for a service licence from Spiggie to Lerwick. However, he only operated this service on a Thursday and a Saturday afternoon. This supplemented the afternoon service operated by Ganson Brothers into Lerwick on Tuesdays and Fridays; between them, Moncrieff and Ganson's were the only ones who operated an afternoon service into Lerwick from the Southern Mainland. He sold out to A.J. Eunson in 1962.

Reg.	Chassis	Body	Cap.	Year	Acq.
GS 6981	Thornycroft	?	C20F	1936	1948
AMS 339	Bedford OWB	SMT	B26F	1945	1956
SK 2826	Bedford OWB	Duple	B26F	1944	1962

Centre Right Top: *In 1936 this Thornycroft was registered GS 6981. We know little about its early life but the body has a look similar to those produced by J.H. Jennings of Sandbach, Cheshire. It has a C20F body, and generous head room, topped off by a large canvas sun-roof. It was purchased by Moncrieff in 1948 and was scrapped eight years later in 1956.*

Centre Right: *The replacement for the Thornycroft was a Bedford OWB (24683) from 1945, which had a SMT B26F body. This featured the 'relaxed' seating arrangement that came about from February 1945, when the Ministry of War Transport allowed the replacement of wooden-slatted seats, with steel frames and the squabs and backs covered with rexine or leather cloth. Registered AMS 339 it was purchased from P.J. Smith of Sandwick in 1956 and was scrapped in 1962.*

Centre Right Bottom: *SK 2862 also came from P.J. Smith and was acquired in 1962 to replace AMS 339. It was a Bedford OWB (21535) but the body is unusual. It is either a modified Duple Service Bus body or a re-built OWB. This was the final bus in the fleet and was sold to A.J. Eunson in November 1964.*

J. MORRISON

Based in Bigton, little is known about the operation run by John Morrison. He ran a restricted service from Bigton to Lerwick, but as far as we know he only ever operated one bus of 13 or more seats. This was a Bedford WLB, with a Duple C20F body dating from 1934. Registered PO 7619 (pictured left) it was purchased from Leask's of Lerwick in 1948, and remained in operation until the business was taken over by A.J. Eunson in June 1952.

E.M.B. JOHNSON

Operating from Bigton, the locally renowned Elizabeth Johnson (better known as Elma) purchased this Ford Transit (BDVESE08082) with a Ford Conversion 14-seat interior in 1997. The 1995-built M990 GHS came from Murchisons of Aberdeen and was purchased mainly for school runs. In addition Elma operates some feeder services in the Bigton area and also private hire work. In recent years she has started a tour service called Island Trails, which takes small groups all over Shetland on guided tours.

IRVINE BROTHERS

This business was founded by Alex Irvine of Boddam, who owned a croft and a butchers shop. He had four sons, William, Alex, John and Morris. The sons joined the father in the family business which included a small car hire operation. It seems that their first vehicle was a Model T Ford, which was adapted for passenger and goods carrying. By 1935 the business was purely in the name of William Irvine and the following year he purchased his first big bus, a 14-seat Chevrolet. Another vehicle, a Bedford WLB, was purchased during World War II to replace the Chevrolet. In 1961 the traffic commissioners received a change of name for the business to Irvine Brothers, at which time the firm were listed as having one public service route from Quendale to Lerwick. After William Irvine died the business was wound down and the last remaining vehicle became a mobile mission.

Reg.	Chassis	Body	Cap.	Year	Acq.
ST 6565	Chevrolet	?	B14F	1931	1936
RV 1078	Bedford WLB	Duple?	C20F	1933	1942
SB 6705	Bedford OB	Duple	C27F	1947	1949
PS 1977	Bedford OB	Mulliner	DP28F	1950	New
FAO 822	Bedford OWB	SMT	B28F	1945	1955
FFS 887	Bedford OB	SMT	C25F	1948	1961
FDK 570	Bedford OB	Duple	C27F	1947	1961

Above: *Pictured with his last vehicle, Bedford OB (FFS 887), William Irvine is seen on the right, with driver Jamie Bolt,.*

Centre Left: *The first bus belonging to what is called Irvine's Motor Service, Dunrossness. This was registered ST 6565 and was a Chevrolet (71597), with what appears to be a Hendon motor body (Duple) C14F. It was obtained from MacRae & Dick of Inverness in 1936 and scrapped in 1942.*

Bottom Left: *Bought to replace ST 6565, RV 1078 was a 1933 Bedford WLB purchased from Ardgour of Acharachle in 1942. It*

Left: *The replacement for RV 1078 was the relatively new SB 6705. This Bedford OB (19801) had a Duple Vista C27F body and dated from 1947. It had previously been operated in the Dunoon area and lasted with Irvine bros. until 1961 when it was scrapped. It is seen here passing along a narrow section of Commercial Street in Lerwick in the 1950s.*

Right: *In 1950 the Irvine operation got its only new coach, which was a Bedford OB (137617) with a Mulliner Mk II service bus body (T558). This had 28-seats, which were classed as dual purpose and it also had luggage racks. It stayed at Boddam until 1968, when it was scrapped after 18-years in service.*

Left: *New to an operator in Cumberland, FAO 822 was registered in Carlisle in 1945 and captured here on film by Ken Jubb. It later moved to Ganson Brothers in Lerwick and was purchased by Irvine Bros. in 1955. It was a Bedford OWB with a 'relaxed' SMT body. It is seen pictured here in the Ganson livery of grey and cream with a red stripe. It lasted at Boddam until 1961 when it was scrapped.*

Right: *In 1961 two coaches arrived in Lerwick on the same boat but, due to exceptionally bad weather, they were unable to land and had to be returned to Aberdeen. These were two Bedford OBs purchased from Highland Omnibus, the first of which was FFS 887 (chassis number 76581) with a 25-seat SMT body. Formerly Highland C126 it was eventually landed successfully at Lerwick and remained in service until 1969. Its latter years were not as a PSV however, but as a mobile mission.*

Left: *The other coach purchased from Highland (C125) in 1961 was FDK 570, an OB (40551) with a Duple Vista C27F body (44846). Built in 1947 this coach (and FDK 571) was new to Yelloway of Rochdale, and passed to the ownership of A.J. Eunson at Sumburgh in 1964.*

J.A. & G.D. NICOLSON

Andrew and George Nicolson from Cunningsburgh, began business in 1992 when they obtained a Freight Rover E141 VGG for school work. The firm are still in operation today with two vehicles on school work and private hire, supplemented by a stage carriage service from Sumburgh Airport to Lerwick.

Reg.	Chassis	Body	Cap.	Year	Acq.
E141 VGG	Freight Rover	Williams	C16F	1987	1992
FLD 447Y	Bedford YMP	Plaxton	C35F	1982	1996
K105 YFL	Leyland DAF	Jubilee	C16F	1992	1996
M34 CHS	Mercedes 609D	Crystal	C24F	1995	1998

Above: *Seen next to M34 CHS, is Nicolson's third vehicle K105 YFL. This 16-seat LDV with a Jubilee 16-seat conversion was purchased from Loch Lann Minicoaches, Culloden in 1996.*

Centre Left: *E141 VGG, a Freight Rover Sherpa with a Williams 16-seat body was purchased from Thomson of Milngavie in 1992 and was scrapped in 1995.*

Bottom Left: *Short-lived FLD 447Y, was a Bedford YMP (YMP2DZCT104410) with a Plaxton Supreme C35F body (828MQS5C001) dating from 1982. It was bought from R & I Coaches, Park Royal in anticipation of a larger school run, but this was sold in 1996 having only done a few private hires.*

Bottom Right: *The latest in the fleet M34 CHS, is a Mercedes 609D (WDB6680632-NO-30866), with a Crystal Conversion C24F body (1314) purchased from Fairline Coaches in 1998.*

J.J. & A. LESLIE

We next come to the firm of J.J. & A Leslie who operated a service from Sumburgh into Lerwick, via Scatness, Virkie, Boddam, and Levenwick. They did this run daily except Wednesdays and Sundays, but on a Sunday they did a service from Virkie to Dunrossness Church. Their registered address was North House, Virkie but the name Leslie first appeared in motor vehicle records back in 1923 after a goods lorry was purchased. This was an ex-American Army Model T Ford, which was left-hand drive. Sometime in the 1920s a 1-ton Ford truck was purchased, and it seems as though a demountable coach body was built for this by a joiner in Lerwick. The bus was listed with the traffic commissioners in the late 1920s, but no other details have emerged about what was done in the years leading up to World War II. In 1946 the first 13+ seat vehicle was acquired in the form of a 10-year old Bedford WTB, followed by a similar vehicle in 1947. Three more coaches were purchased in the years that followed, before the business came to an end in 1969.

Reg.	Chassis	Body	Cap.	Year	Acq.
BEA 274	Bedford WTB	Plaxton?	C14F	1936	1946
RG 7800	Bedford WTB	Duple	C25F	1937	1947
WG 5773	Bedford WTB	Duple	C25F	1938	1955
BCB 96	Bedford OB	Plaxton	C30F	1948	1959
SS 7237	Bedford OB	Duple	C29F	1949	1959

Top Left: *BEA 274 was the first bus purchased by Leslie in 1946, it was a WTB chassis which Bedford recorded as a Plaxton C14F; however, the photograph above does not really confirm this. It lasted until 1955 when it was sold for conversion to a mobile shop on Whalsay.*

Top Right: *A year after acquiring BEA 274, another Bedford WTB (111316) was purchased, this time with a Duple C25F body. Dating from 1937, RG 7800 came from Summers of Aberdeen and lasted until 1959 when it was scrapped.*

Centre Right Top: *The replacement for BEA 274, was WG 5773, a Bedford WTB (111080) from 1938. It also had a Duple C25F body and came from Leask's of Lerwick in 1955 and lasted four years before being scrapped in 1959.*

Centre Right Bottom: *Definitely fitted with a Plaxton body was this forward-control Bedford OB (58000) registered BCB 96. As can be seen in the picture it had the full-fronted Plaxton C30F body, which dated from 1948. It was purchased as an 11-year old vehicle from J. Peterson of Ollaberry in 1959. It was withdrawn in December 1966 and later scrapped. As will be seen on pages 8 and 99 it was almost identical to another Leask bus, FBU 149.*

Bottom Right: *The last coach to be purchased, in 1959, was SS 7237. This was a Bedford OB (109966) from Ganson Bros., with a Duple Vista C29F body (54296). When the business ended in May 1969, this was the sole surviving member of the fleet, and it was sold to Pat Isbister at Walls.*

A.J. EUNSON

Commencing in 1952 A.J. Eunson (better known locally as Ally), began his business when he took over the operation of John Morrison of Bigton. This involved the running of a public service from Virkie into Lerwick. In 1964 he went on to absorb two more small businesses, the first of which was J.S. Moncrieff, followed by the Irvine Bros. operation in November 1964. He continued the services from Virkie into Lerwick, but this was to dramatically expand when the oil boom hit Shetland in the early 1970s. At this time he started a private hire service running from Sumburgh Airport to the Sullom Voe site. This was a direct service running the full length of the Mainland, and was probably a round journey of about 120 miles. He did several runs a day and this led to a substantial extension of the fleet. From 1976 onwards he began to give his vehicles names, which was almost unique in Shetland. After the oil construction work declined, he sold the business to John Leask & Sons in October 1983.

Top: *As A.J. Eunson was long associated with oil construction workers transport, we begin this chapter with a picture of this firm's buses at Sullom Voe in 1981.*

Centre Left: *The very first bus to be purchased by A.J. Eunson was PO 7619, which came from J. Morrison of Bigton in June 1952 and is pictured here in the livery of John Leask & Sons. This was a 1934 Bedford WLB with a Duple C20F body, so at the age of 20-years it is not surprising that it had a very short life with Eunson and was scrapped in 1956.*

Bottom Left: *Its replacement was a Bedford WTB (111074) with a Duple 20-seat body, registered WG 5772. This came from Alan Leask of Aith in 1956 and was scrapped in 1963.*

Over the years the fleet of A.J. Eunson was as follows:-

Reg.	Chassis	Body	Cap.	Year	Acq.
PO 7819	Bedford WLB	Duple	C20F	1934	1952
WG 5772	Bedford WTB	Duple	C20F	1938	1956
MPT 410	Bedford OB	Duple	C29F	1951	1959
SK 2562	Bedford OWB	Duple	B26F	1944	1962
FDK 570	Bedford OB	Duple	C27F	1947	1964
HMS 226	Bedford SBG	Burlingham	C35F	1956	1968
SGB 355	Bedford SBG	Duple	C41F	1956	1969
8329 U	AEC Reliance	Plaxton	C41C	1958	1970
KWX 440	Bedford SB	Duple	C33F	1951	1971
588 UTJ	Ford 570E	Duple	C41F	1960	1972
903 CDU	Ford 570E	Duple	C41F	1964	1973
SGB 359	Bedford SGB	Duple	C41F	1956	1975
633 WKL	AEC Reliance	Harrington	C45F	1963	1976
JAR 614G	AEC Reliance	Plaxton	C51F	1969	1976
SCL 62J	Bedford YRQ	Duple	C45F	1971	1976
EUS 963C	Ford 676E	Plaxton	C52F	1965	1976
URF 559C	Bedford SB5	Duple	C41F	1965	1976
LVO 92E	AEC Reliance	Plaxton	C53F	1967	1977
PGM 639H	Bedford VAM70	Duple	C45F	1970	1977
EMA 461K	Seddon	Plaxton	C53F	1972	1978
VYH 499M	Bedford YRQ	Plaxton	C45F	1974	1978
NAR 401L	Bedford VAS5	Duple	C29F	1973	1978
JPT 774N	Bedford YRQ	Duple	C45F	1974	1978
DJG 609C	AEC Reliance	Park Royal	DP49F	1965	1978
HAY 777L	Bedford YRQ	Duple	C45F	1973	1980
MPS 901W	Bedford YLQ	Plaxton	C45F	1980	New

Top Right: *The third bus to be acquired, this time from Johnson of Scalloway in 1959, was MPT 410. This Bedford OB (146361) with a Duple Vista C29F body (56618) was in service with Eunson until as late as 1976, when it was sold for spares at the age of 25-years.*

Centre Right Top: *This late model OB (MPT 410) ended up on Whalsay and lay derelict for some time, during which some wit wrote the following poem on its side:-*

  I'm just a poor lonely bus,
  My seats have been stripped,
  I'm speckled with rust,
  My service has ended I'm needed no more,
  I stand here in silence,
  Just a great big eyesore.

Centre Right Bottom: *In 1962 Eunson took over the Moncrieff service and acquired SK 2562. This has been listed as a Bedford OWB chassis (21535), but it does not have the standard Duple utility body. This colour picture further emphasises the possibility of this being a postwar re-build, but further details would be welcomed by the author. In 1966 this unusual vehicle was scrapped at the age of 22-years.*

Bottom Right: *As you may recall, FDK 570 was one of the vehicles purchased from Highland Omnibus (C125) and twice made the journey from Aberdeen to Lerwick. A Duple Vista C27F body (44866) on an OB chassis (40551), it was built in 1947 and acquired when Eunson bought out Irvine Bros. in November 1964. The coach lasted just four more years and was scrapped in 1966.*

Above: *New to the Leeds firm of Wallace Arnold Tours in 1958, 8329 U was an AEC Reliance (MU3RA1953). As will be seen from the above picture the vehicle was given a Plaxton Consort II C41C body (2174). It will also be noted that, in addition to the centre door arrangement, this coach has an abundance of roof light windows; it has six full-sized (and one small cant) rail windows on each side, and two roof quarter lights. This must have made for a very light and airy coach, ideal for sight-seeing and tour work. The AEC chassis and power unit would also have provided a very strong and powerful coach with this size of body. This vehicle was the eighth member of the Eunson fleet and was purchased from Rennie of Dunfermline in April 1970 and scrapped in 1975.*

Centre Left: *Still bearing the livery of Alexander Northern, the next acquisition's paintwork was still in good condition on arrival, and it was left unpainted for economy measures. This coach, HMS 226, was Alexander fleet number NW259, a Bedford SBG (46978) with a body built by the Blackpool firm of H.V. Burlingham (6306) in 1956. It was purchased in March 1968 and scrapped in 1973, however it did leave a legacy in the fleet, in that the yellow and cream livery was adopted for later acquisitions by Eunson.*

Bottom Left: *In July 1969 the firm purchased SGB 355 from Easton of Inverurie. This was a Bedford SBG (50042) with a Duple Super Vega C41F body (1074/215). The attractive finish of this coach with its side-flashes and 'Butterfly Grill' is shown off well by the yellow and cream colour scheme that Eunson applied. Seen here after a working to Sumburgh, this coach would last until 1976 when it was scrapped.*

Top Right: *Another acquisition by Eunson also originated in the West Riding of Yorkshire, as KWX 440 was new to Balme of Otley at the end of August 1951. This Duple Vega C33F (1006/256) was built on the Bedford SB chassis number 3370. It was some 20-years old when purchased from Harry Wood of North Roe, but it managed a further seven years for Eunson before it was scrapped in 1978.*

Centre Right: *Sadly this very poor photograph of 588 UTJ is the only picture I have been able to find of this 1960-built coach. It has the Ford Thames 570E chassis (510E66156) with a Duple Yeoman C41F body (1184/301). It was acquired by Eunson in October 1972 from Easton of Inverurie. As will be noted, this was the second vehicle to be purchased by Eunson from that operator, but it only lasted for six years and was scrapped in 1978.*

Below: *A second Ford Thames 570E chassis (L80B831015) was obtained in October 1973 from Stewart of Partington. On this vehicle (903 CDU) the body was a Duple Trooper C41F (1160/87) dating from 1964, which was scrapped in 1981.*

Left: *A second Super Vega C41F (0174/218) on a Bedford SGB chassis (50097) was obtained in September 1975 from Pat Isbister of Walls. Registered SGB 359 this coach dated from 1956 and lasted until 1977 when it was scrapped.*

Right: *Still wearing the livery of Premier Travel, this AEC Reliance 590 (2MU3RA4773) was number 208 in the fleet of this Cambridge operator. The Harrington Cavalier 36 (2796) had 45-seats and was new in 1963. It came to Eunson in 1976 and was stolen from Sullom Voe in 1981 whilst parked up overnight. The thief got as far as Tingwall where he ran it off the road and turned it onto its side, completely wrecking the vehicle.*

Left: *Given the name* Venus *by Eunson, JAR 614G was an AEC Reliance (6U3ZR7267) with a Plaxton Panorama Elite C51F body from 1969. It came from Cheshunt in April 1977, and was sold to John Leask & Son in 1983.*

Right: *Obtained from Mayne's of Buckie, this early Bedford YRQ (IT483772) was fitted with a Duple Viceroy C45F body (227/109). Built in 1971, SLC 62J was purchased by Eunson in July 1976 and written off after being wrecked following a road traffic accident in 1981.*

Left: *A contrasting pair of Bedford coaches in the Eunson fleet, pictured in 1976. Both vehicles MPT 410 (on the left) and SCL 62J (on the right) have featured earlier in this chapter, but side by side, the two present an interesting contrast in Bedford-Duple coaches. Some 20-years separated the two, and at the time of this picture the OB was already a quarter of century old!*

Right: *Another coach from the Eunson fleet to prove elusive when it comes to photographs, was EUS 963C as this was only in the fleet a very short time. It was acquired from Miller of Larkhall in 1976, and wrecked following an accident that same year. The only real picture of this Ford 676E (L80D437695) shows it after its accident. When it crashed the Plaxton Panorama C52F body (652587) was badly damaged and, at 11-years old, repair was uneconomical. As will be noted, it was never repainted in the Eunson livery.*

Left: *Another 1965-built coach, URF 559C, entered the fleet in 1976. Purchased in August from O'Neill of Glasgow, this was a Bedford SB5 (95556) with a Duple Bella Vega 41-seat body (1183/106). It is seen here in the colours of its former owners, sometime before it was withdrawn and scrapped in 1978.*

Right: *New to Central Coaches of Padiham in 1967, LVO 92E was one of a fleet of coaches operated by this Lancashire firm on 'camping holidays' to France, Italy, Switzerland and Spain in the late-1960s. The red, cream and green livery was complimented by the lettering 'Central Angleterre' on the side. This AEC Reliance (6U2R6834) was purchased from Smith of Tysoe in January 1977 and named* Apollo *by Eunson It remained in the fleet until 1983, although it was scrapped before the firm was acquired by Leask's of Lerwick.*

Left: *Continuing the 'planet-theme', when PGM 639H was purchased in April 1977, it was given the name* Uranus. *It was new to Central SMT in 1970, and became their fleet number C39. A Bedford VAM 70 (0T477568), the Duple Viceroy-bodied C45F (211/31) was retained until November 1983 when it too was purchased by John Leask. It is shown here in Lerwick, with driver Lowrie Moar.*

Right: *Here EMA 461K, a Seddon Pennine IV (51590) is seen parked in front of LVO 92E. Dating from 1972, this Plaxton Panorama Elite (729447) had a seating capacity of 53. Coming from Mair of Bucksburn in February 1978 (along with NAR 40L), this coach was sold to Bolts in May 1983.*

Left: *On the occasion of the open day at Sullom Voe, Aries (VYH 499M) provides transportation for visiting families. This was a Bedford YRQ (CW451947) with a Plaxton Panorama Elite III C53F body (7410QC011) dating from 1974 when it was new to National Travel (South East). It was purchased by Eunson at the end of 1978, but delivered in April 1979, and was eventually sold to John Leask & Son in November 1983.*

Right: *Named* Adventure *by A.J. Eunson,NAR 401L was a Bedford VAS (CW453431) dating from 1973. It was another vehicle to come from Mair of Bucksburn in February 1978, and it would leave the island in 1983 when it was sold to the dealers Caledonia. Later on this 29-seat Duple Vista25 (263/1753) was reported as being used by the Christian Centre Ministries in Glasgow.*

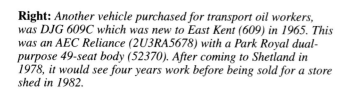

Left: *Registered in Sunderland in 1974, JPT 774N joined the Eunson fleet from Willoughby of Jarrow in September 1978. This Bedford YRQ (EW450672) had a Duple Dominant C45F body (515/2005) and was named* Executive. *It passed to Leask's in November 1983*

Right: *Another vehicle purchased for transport oil workers, was DJG 609C which was new to East Kent (609) in 1965. This was an AEC Reliance (2U3RA5678) with a Park Royal dual-purpose 49-seat body (52370). After coming to Shetland in 1978, it would see four years work before being sold for a store shed in 1982.*

Left: *There are no rings to be seen around* Saturn *in this picture, but the planetary name theme was continued on HAY 777L. This Duple Dominant C45F (266/32) was fitted to a Bedford YRQ chassis (CW452172) in 1973. It came from Woods of Wigston in August 1980, and passed to Bolts Coaches in 1983.*

Above: *Here we see the bright star in the Eunson fleet, Sirus, which was the only new coach ever bought by this operator. Registered MPS 901W, this Bedford YLQ (KW452859) came to Shetland in 1980, and was fitted with a Plaxton Supreme IV C45F body (8010QX5095). It was another of the fleet to be purchased by Leask's in 1983.*

Below; *Not part of the Eunson fleet, but logically located at the end of that chapter for geographic reasons, we see LVS 440V. This 1980 Leyland Leopard (7903683) was purchased by Highland & Island Airways for use at Sumburgh Airport as an emergency support vehicle. It had a Plaxton Supreme IV C53F body (8011LC029) and has been in Shetland since 1997.*

At this stage in the book, having covered all the bus companies one by one, I would have liked to say something about the services they each operated, but as you can imagine that would take a book in its own right. So for a point of interest I thought that I would quote the opening paragraphs of a magazine article written in *Buses Illustrated* by G. R. Croughton in 1965 entitled *The Shetland Bus*, even though this is not entirely accurate it does make very interesting reading.

'On the same latitude as Southern Greenland and as near to Bergen in Norway as to Aberdeen, the Shetland Islands constitute the most northerly outpost of the British Isles. Known as Mainland, the largest of the islands measures 50 miles from north to south and is some 25 miles wide at its mid-point, although for the most part much narrower. The heather-covered hills are so deeply penetrated by fjord-like "voes" that nowhere is more than 2 1/4 miles from the sea, and at one point near Brae the Atlantic Ocean and the North Sea are little more than 50 yards apart.

Road distances are increased by unavoidable detours around the heads of these voes and speed is restricted by frequent changes of gradient and sharp corners. Although many roads are single track with passing places, the majority are well surfaced and quite adequate for the traffic which they bear. ....'

Above: *Here we show a typical Bedford scene on the Isle of Yell, with R. G. Jamieson's YJ 8939 and T.R. Manson's ERG 164 at the changeover point on the 'Overland Service' at Mid-Yell.*

Centre Left: *In the Western Mainland we see a line up of buses at Walls.*

Bottom Left: *Another view taken at Mid-Yell, this time with BKS 179 and YJ 8939.*

Top Right: *Typical summer tours operated around Shetland in the 1950s and 1960s witnessed scenes like this featuring PS 2627, SY 9964, PS 2001, KWX 412 and PS 1927 at the Market Cross, Lerwick in 1957.*

Centre Right: *Bus services from the town were not always in the most comfortable of vehicles, and here we see a couple of examples in the form of Johnson Bros. NGY 823 and Garriock's SMY 140, which are waiting to leave with return workings from Lerwick.*

Below: *The fleet of James Johnson & Son from Scalloway in the late 1950s showing, from left to right the drivers Hind Johnson, Louis Johnson, Bob Johnson (all three brothers), followed by Alex Mout, Lowrie Humphray and a young Larry Sutherland.*

The article continued:- 'The total population has declined from 21,400 in 1931 to the present figure of 18,700, of whom 5,600 live in Lerwick, principal port and commercial centre of the islands, situated in a sheltered position on the east coast overlooking Bressay to which it is linked by a regular ferry service. Fishing, mostly trawling, crofting and knitting are the main means of livelihood so that apart from the shops and some light industrial plants in Lerwick there are few employers and little daily travel to and from work, although school contracts are an important feature for some bus operators. Only one of the 13 stage carriage operators is based at Lerwick. Most of the remainder make a morning journey into town from the outlying districts and return from Lerwick at 1700 or 1800. The majority of these services run at least four days a week and one or two include Sunday operation but none function on a Wednesday which is early closing day in Lerwick.'

I have to say that I have had a great degree of fun in compiling this book, despite the fact that our aim to get it completed and published has run in to all kinds of problems. A bad ankle injury whilst travelling south with the pictures for the book considerably slowed up progress, and at the time of writing I am still sat here with my whole leg in plaster. The problems that this caused for my publisher can well be imagined and at the 11th hour, Alan Earnshaw travelled up to Shetland to help me with it. But even then this was compounded by the severe gales of November 2000, followed by a few gremlins creeping into the computer systems just before we went to print.

But would I do it all again? Well probably not, for it has taken me a lifetime to collect this batch of photographic material, and it has also cost a small fortune to do it. My desire to make this book all-colour has also required a major financial input. For Trans-Pennine to produce a book of this scope and quality at a very modest cover price has also been a major contribution, with Alan, Larraine, Matthew, Bryony, and Louise all working many hours in order to make it happen. And then thanks go to Robert Berry, Peter Leask and Larry Sutherland for checking the text.

The help of my fiance, Sandra Smith has been absolutely vital, and without her love, advice and generous support, I know that this book would have remained in the realms of fantasy! I also hope that you (the reader) will appreciate all that has gone into it. So as for the future, well I am collecting pictures of trucks that have worked in Shetland, and if you can help me here, I'd be really grateful, but as for another book.........only time will tell.

Above: *BJX 848C and FBU 149 on Mid-Yell pier seen when working the Overland Service.*

Centre Left: *Again on the Overland Service, but this time at Ulsta, ERG 164, KWX 412 and BPS 987K await the ferry.*

Bottom Left: *Consecutively registered Bedfords, but sporting Duple and Plaxton bodies, L. G. Jamieson's HPS 28P and Leask's HPS 27P stand at the Ulsta Ferry Terminal when new.*

In conclusion, may I again say how grateful I am to all those who have helped me trace this history, and the pages that have preceded this one is a testament to the help of hundreds of people. We have had a large number of pictures showing Bedford buses and coaches as 162 Bedfords saw service in Shetland, five times the number of the nearest rival Ford. Traditional heavyweights like AEC and Leyland, between them, only accounted for 23 vehicles, whilst in more recent times Volvo have supplied 26. The chart below will give a clear indication of the breakdown of vehicle types and numbers, and I hope it presents some useful statistics.

Austin	9	Guy	2
Aec	10	Iveco	2
Albion	2	Karrier	1
Bedford	162	Leyland	13
Bristol	2	Morris Commercial	1
Chevrolet	6	Man	5
Citroen	1	Mercedes	17
Commer	1	MCW	2
Daf	9	Renault	2
Daimler	1	Reo	2
Dennis	6	Scania	1
Dodge	2	Seddon	1
Fiat	2	Thornycroft	3
Ford	32	Talbot	4
Fordson	6	Volvo	26
Freight Rover	3	**Total**	**337**

Top Right: *Lined up together RPS 380Y, HPS 27P, A416 SPS, KPS 701T and MGE 88Y are seen on the corner above Scalloway during a cruise liner tour.*

Centre Right: *Next we see HPS 27P, OPS 742X and RPS 380Y on the pier at Lerwick also during a cruise liner tour.*

Below: *A line up of coaches at Cullivoe, three of which we endeavoured to save as a little piece of our past destined for the enjoyment of future generations.*

And finally:- *Two OBs run by the Trustees of T.R. Manson of West Sandwick (FBU 493 and ERG 164) are being driven through deep snow by Lowrie Spence and Lell Robertson in this glorious picture at Burravoe, Yell in the winter of 1969.*

Although this book carries my name and the imprint of Trans-Pennine Publishing it is safe to say that this work could not have been carried out without the help of a large number of people. Some helped in a small way, but this often filled in a vital part of the jigsaw; others offered substantial help and advice that was really vital. Many people have loaned me photographs, including several bus drivers, like Ken Jubb of Midland Red and Don Spriggs of Wallace Arnold, who visited Shetland in the 1960s and 1970s. Several enthusiasts came to visit our garage or travel on our buses and I have since kept in touch with them. Where possible I also arranged to buy copies of photographs they took while they were in the Isles and quite a few of these have been included in this book. Other pictures came from anonymous donors, or were passed on 'second-hand', but to all those who have supplied pictures, may I say a heartfelt thank you!

Speaking of the collection of photographs I have built up over the years, a very special thank you must go to my good friend Brian Duncan. He has spent countless hours (probably amounting to weeks or months in total), wading through the mounds of paper I presented to him. From this chaos he made a record of chassis and body numbers. This has been invaluable to me and comprises a great part of this book. His hard work and loyal friendship are greatly appreciated.

I must also thank the late-Jim Nicolson of Brindister, as I had the privilege of spending many hours in his company during the 1980s, literally picking his brain for the wealth of knowledge he had on the history of every operator from Lerwick, Scalloway and the South Mainland. He had a remarkable memory, which I can only liken to a modern-day computer. He was able to provide me with registration numbers of some buses when even their owners could not remember them. I never felt the need to question any of these. It was only many years after his death that I obtained photographs from an enthusiast who had been holidaying in Shetland during the 1950s. These clearly showed the registration numbers exactly as Jim had remembered them. He was what I would call brilliant. I am deeply indebted to him and I will never forget this truly unique man.

My thanks must also go to Peter Leask for his help with the complete history of his family business. I would like to thank him for this and also the many photos he loaned to me. His brother, Andrew, has also played an important part in keenly supporting the project.

Of course it would be unfair just to single out the firm of John Leask & Sons, for over the many years I have gained a great deal of help, advice and information from operators, drivers, and enthusiasts from all over Shetland. In the course of the numerous conversations with them I was told many amusing or fascinating stories. I would have loved to put many of these into print, but in the end did not dare to: if you know what I mean! However, it will always give me a great deal of pleasure and amusement when recalling them.

Many other groups and bodies have helped considerably, including the PSV Circle (particularly Ernest Burnett of Glasgow) who supplied much detail regarding body and chassis numbers and filled in some of the missing gaps. Richard Gadsby supplied, almost at the 11th-hour, some vital new information, whilst my friend (the well known Scottish transport historian) Robert Grieves was highly supportive.

In Lerwick the local museum has been splendid, and whilst bus operation may only fill a small part of the rich tapestry of Shetland Heritage, the museum were helpful and enthusiastic.

I must also acknowledge Shetland Island Tourism who supplied the map at the front of the book. I am sure that they will be equally helpful to any one who wishes to visit us in the Northern Isles. Other parties have also helped with our attempts to preserve some of the old buses from Shetland, especially P&O Scottish Ferries. However, for a large part this work has been a labour of love undertaken without any official assistance whatsoever! So I must most sincerely thank Professor Alan Earnshaw of Trans-Pennine Publishing, not only for his enthusiasm, expertise and extreme hard work, but most especially his friendship and hospitality. I can never repay him. To Alan, Larraine and their family (who between them form the basis of Trans-Pennine Publishing) thank you.